Inheritance Tax Made Simple

The essential guide to understanding inheritance tax

by Andrew Komarnyckyj

Hh

HARRIMAN HOUSE LTD

3A Penns Road
Petersfield
Hampshire
GU32 2EW
GREAT BRITAIN

Tel: +44 (0)1730 233870
Fax: +44 (0)1730 233880
Email: enquiries@harriman-house.com
Website: www.harriman-house.com

First published in Great Britain in 2011

ISBN: 978-0-85719-020-8

British Library Cataloguing in Publication Data
A CIP catalogue record for this book can be obtained from the British Library.

Printed and bound in Great Britain by CPI Antony Rowe

Disclaimer

Please note that this book does not replace the need to take legal and/or financial advice from a qualified expert when making tax-planning arrangements. Indeed, this book recommends that such advice is sought and taken.

Every effort has been made to ensure that the contents of the book are accurate when going to press. However the accuracy of the contents cannot be guaranteed. Inheritance tax, like all taxes, is frequently subject to change.

The publisher and author and any company or individual involved in the sale or distribution of the book cannot accept responsibility for loss occasioned to any person through acting, or failing to act, as a result of relying on the contents.

Contents

About the Author

Andrew Komarnyckyj is the director of a niche legal practice delivering innovative legal services to the public and to other professionals. He had a successful career in sales and marketing prior to qualifying as a solicitor.

He studied law by correspondence course while working full-time, and was awarded two prizes for achieving the highest marks nationally in one of his law exams.

During his legal career he has been the head of the probate department for two leading West Yorkshire firms of solicitors, at one of which he became a partner. He has over 15 years' legal experience working exclusively in the field of wills, trusts, tax planning and probate.

He left conventional legal employment in March 2009 in order to establish Wills, Probate and More (**www.willsprobateandmore.co.uk**), his own niche legal services company, and to be free to comment on the legal profession as an outsider. He now divides his time between legal practice and writing. Andrew is also the author of *Probate Made Simple* (Harriman House, 2010).

Abbreviations

For a detailed glossary, see Appendix 3 on page 188.

AIM	Alternative Investment Market
APR	agricultural property relief
BPR	business property relief
CP	civil partner/civil partnership
CGT	capital gains tax
DOV	deeds of variation
EEA	European Economic Area
FLIT	flexible life interest trust
GROB	gift with a reservation of benefit
HMRC	Her Majesty's Revenue & Customs
IFA	independent financial advisor
IHT	inheritance tax
IHTA	Inheritance Tax Act
IIP	interest in possession
IPDI	immediate post-death interest
NICs	National Insurance Contributions
NRB	nil-rate band
PET	potentially exempt transfer
POAT	pre-owned assets tax
PR	personal representative
USM	Unlisted Securities Market
VOA	Valuation Office Agency

Preface

The main aims of this book are:

1. to help you to understand inheritance tax (IHT) and how it could impact on you and your family (Part 1)
2. to detail options you may have for reducing the burden of inheritance tax, set out in a practical way that is accessible to the general reader (Part 2 and 3)
3. to help you to get the most from your tax advisor – whether you use a solicitor, accountant or Independent Financial Advisor (IFA) – if you engage one (Part 4).

Note that inheritance tax may be imposed on all of your assets worldwide if you are domiciled in the United Kingdom (UK), and on your UK assets even if you are not domiciled in the UK. This applies to all areas of the UK, i.e. England, Wales, Scotland and Northern Ireland.

Understanding IHT

With regard to (1) and (2) above, many people will not find it necessary to have a comprehensive knowledge of the IHT regime in order to understand how IHT will impact on them and what measures they might take to mitigate the tax. For example, if you do not own a farm and you are unlikely ever to own farmland, you may not need to get to grips with the concept of agricultural property relief.

However, the majority of people reading this book should nevertheless acquaint themselves with Part 1 before reading the other sections that deal with tax planning, the administration of estates, and so on. In particular, all readers should consider and understand the following before even considering the tax planning content of the book:

- The Executive Overview of Inheritance Tax Regime (page xvi)
- IHT in a nutshell (transfers of value) (1.2) (page 2)
- The nil-rate band and the rate of IHT (1.5) (page 7)

- The spouse/civil partner exemption (1.8) (page 10)
- The transferable nil-rate band (1.9) (page 12)

If you read this book before seeing a tax advisor (even if you read only the narrative text and do not bother going through all the calculations) it is likely that you will save your advisor time explaining things to you; you will also have a better appreciation of his proposals (and may even have a few of your own), and will probably save money in legal and/or accountancy fees (typically charged out at upwards of £200 per hour for this kind of advice).

Inheriting wealth

If you are a beneficiary in a will (or under an intestacy, i.e. where there is no will) and you are due to receive inherited wealth that is subject to inheritance tax, there is often nothing that can be done to mitigate the situation. However, there are circumstances in which action is possible and this book will draw your attention to some of the circumstances in which you will have opportunities to reduce or eliminate the tax on your inheritance.

Administering an estate

If you are an executor or administrator and you are administering an estate that may be subject to inheritance tax, this book will help you and possibly save you money by signposting the main problems that could arise.

Calculations of IHT made in this book

There is an exemption from inheritance tax known as the £3,000 annual exemption (explained at 1.16.1.1). This has been ignored in the calculations, in order to make the calculations clear and easy to follow.

References

The legal basis for IHT is set out in an Act of Parliament called the Inheritance Tax Act 1984 (IHTA 1984). This has been added to and amended over the years by a number of other acts known as Finance Acts. In addition, the tax has been shaped by legal cases in which taxpayers have appealed against decisions made by Her Majesty's Revenue & Customs (HMRC).

HMRC has issued manuals to provide guidance to tax inspectors. One such manual is the HMRC *Inheritance Tax Manual*, which can be accessed online (at **www.hmrc.gov.uk**) by the taxpayer. It provides useful information on (amongst other things) the HMRC interpretation of tax law*.

On occasion, the IHTA 1984 and the HMRC manual have been cited where it is thought that they might be of interest, or shed some light on a particular point being made.

Inheritance tax touches some of the most sensitive areas of any legal subject, and dealing with it can often be unduly stressful, or come at a difficult time in the life of yourself or of loved ones. It is my hope that this book is a helpfully straightforward and thorough guide to this complex area of law, and that it lessens such stresses as far as is possible.

Andrew Komarnyckyj

Huddersfield, 2010

---

*Subject to the following caveats:

"... it should not be assumed that the guidance is comprehensive nor that it will provide a definitive answer in every case. HMRC are expected to use their own judgement, based on their training and experience, in applying the guidance to the facts of particular cases. In particular difficult or complex cases they are able to obtain further guidance from specialists in Head Office.

"The guidance in these manuals is based on the law as it stood at date of publication. HMRC will publish amended or supplementary guidance if there is a change in the law or in the Department's interpretation of it. HMRC may give earlier notice of such changes through *Tax Bulletin* or a press release.

"Subject to these qualifications readers may assume that the guidance given will be applied in the normal case; but where HMRC considers that there is, or may have been, avoidance of tax the guidance will not necessarily apply.

"Neither this guidance nor its publication affects any right of appeal a taxpayer may have..." (Quoted from the *Introduction to Her Majesty's Revenue & Customs' Guidance Manuals*.)

Introduction

Inheritance tax was introduced by the Inheritance Tax Act 1984, which came into effect in 1986. It replaced a similar tax regime known as Capital Transfer Tax, which itself was the successor tax to Estate Duty.

It could be argued that inheritance tax is not a tax of any great importance to the UK economy. The tax take it delivers is low in comparison with some other taxes, and it amounts to a very small proportion of the overall tax take. For instance, in the year 2009-10, inheritance tax raised £2,396 million. This sounds impressive until other taxes are considered – income tax raised £144,881 million; National Insurance Contributions (NICs) raised £95,519 million.

The overall tax take in the UK (including NICs) in 2009-2010 was £408,496*. Inheritance tax accounted for only 0.586% of this figure.

Despite this, inheritance tax is important politically. There is probably no other tax that sets out so overtly to tax wealth. The very name of the tax is probably anathema to many people (it has often been popularly renamed the 'Death Tax').

In the year that this book was written (2010) inheritance tax came into the public eye due to a number of developments. The UK economy was said to be in a parlous state, with an excessive budget deficit. One of the measures taken by the Labour government to address this situation (announced in March 2010) was the retention of the inheritance tax nil-rate band at the level of £325,000 for the next four years. The nil-rate band (NRB) is the amount of an estate exempt from paying inheritance tax, and normally rises every year roughly in line with inflation; it had been set to rise to £350,000 in the year 2010-2011.

---

*The figures in this section are all taken from official HM Revenue and Customs statistics.

During their election campaign the Conservative Party included in their manifesto a proposal to increase the nil-rate band to £1,000,000, but the election result left them unable to put the proposal into effect. Their plans on inheritance tax featured amongst the compromises with their coalition partner, the Liberal Democrats.

Given the acknowledged need to put the country's finances in order, it appears likely that inheritance tax will remain at the present level for the duration of the current government. But please don't hold me to that!

Executive Overview of the Inheritance Tax Regime

The aim of this overview is to give you a working knowledge of inheritance tax (IHT) with the least amount of reading needed on your part.

- Inheritance tax is a tax that tends to be charged on wealth given away by someone, mainly when it is given away on death.
- In some circumstances it may be charged on gifts made during a person's lifetime.
- The charge on death is imposed at the time of death (however, a period of grace is permitted in which to allow the executors of the deceased to raise funds to pay the tax).
- The charge on a gift made during the deceased's lifetime (simply, a 'lifetime gift') is imposed at the time the gift is made, if the gift is made into a trust rather than to another individual. Such a gift is called a 'chargeable transfer'. An additional charge may be imposed on a chargeable transfer if the donor of the gift dies within seven years of making it. If the gift is made to another individual rather than to a trust, it is referred

to as a 'potentially exempt transfer' (or PET) and tax will only be payable on it if the donor of the gift dies within seven years of making the gift.

- On death, the first £325,000 in value of the money, property and assets owned by a deceased person (known as his "estate") is tax-free. The tax-free amount is known as the nil-rate band.
- Anything above the nil-rate band figure of £325,000 is taxed at the rate of 40%. E.g. if a person died in October 2009 leaving an estate of £425,000, the IHT that would be payable would be £40,000. (40% of £100,000).
- The nil-rate band figure changes from time to time, usually annually to reflect inflation (see Appendix 1).
- Lifetime gifts made within the seven years prior to death are added to the death estate and subjected to inheritance tax. E.g. if the person in the above example had made a gift of £100,000 to his son in September 2009, the gift would be added to his estate for inheritance tax purposes, producing a taxable amount of £525,000 and a liability to inheritance tax of £80,000.
- In exceptional circumstances (explained in 1.15.5) lifetime gifts made within 14 years prior to death may be added to the death estate and subject to IHT.
- The nil-rate band figure is usually increased each year.
- Because of the state of the economy and the need to raise taxes, the NRB may remain at the current level of £325,000 for some years to come.
- Lifetime gifts and transfers of estates between spouses and civil partners are free of IHT. This is known as the spouse exemption. (E.g. if a husband were to die and leave his wife £100,000,000, this would be tax-free because of the spouse exemption). Exception: if the spouse/civil partner is not UK-domiciled, the spouse exemption is limited to £55,000.

- The nil-rate band can be used up by a person during his or her lifetime. If it is used up, there will be no nil-rate band available on his or her death. It will be used up if that person makes gifts during the last seven years of his or her life which amount in total to the value of the nil-rate band or more than the value of the nil-rate band. If the gifts add up to less than the value of the nil-rate band, the nil-rate band will be partly used up. Gifts by a non-UK domiciled individual to a spouse or civil partner where the spouse or civil partner is UK-domiciled will not use up or reduce the nil-rate band, nor will gifts to UK charities and political parties.
- If the deceased is a surviving spouse or civil partner, his or her executors/administrators may be able to claim any unused nil-rate band of his or her predeceased spouse or civil partner. E.g. Tom died in September 2009 with a full nil-rate band because he had not made any gifts. Tom's wife Cecile, who had also not made any gifts, died in 2005 with a full nil-rate band and left her entire estate to Tom. Tom's executors/administrators should be able to use Tom's nil-rate band of £325,000 and transfer the unused nil-rate band of Cecile to use against the value of his estate, so that Tom's estate gets the benefit of £650,000 free of IHT. (Two nil-rate bands of £325,000 each).
- If a person makes a gift to a trust or to a company during his lifetime, this will usually be a chargeable transfer. This means that, if the gift exceeds the nil-rate band, the value of the gift above the nil-rate band is immediately chargeable to IHT at half the lifetime rate (currently 20%, i.e. half the 40% referred to above). If the person who made the gift dies within seven years of making it, further tax may become payable on the gift. If he survives the gift by seven years, no further tax will be payable.
- If a person makes a gift to another individual during his lifetime, this will be a PET. This means that, if the value of the gift exceeds the nil-rate band and he survives for seven years after making the gift, no tax will be payable on it. If he dies

within seven years, IHT will be payable. However, his executors/administrators may not have to pay the full charge to tax. They may be entitled to relief (known as 'taper relief') depending on how long the donor survived after making the gift (as explained in detail in 1.15.3).

- Lifetime gifts that are not taxable on death are:
    - gifts of less than £3,000 in value *made in any one year* (or £6,000 in value if the £3,000 from the previous year has not been used)
    - normal expenditure out of income (e.g. the payment of school fees or premiums on life insurance policies or on occasion money paid to support someone else)
    - gifts of £250 or less to different beneficiaries
    - gifts to UK charities and political parties (gifts and transfers of estates to UK charities and political parties are free of IHT, whether they take place on death or as lifetime gifts).
- There are various exemptions and reliefs available, e.g. business property relief (BPR – dealt with at 1.17.1), available at the rate of 100% on some business assets and at 50% on some other business assets. Agricultural property relief (APR – dealt with at 1.17.4) is available at the rate of 100% on the agricultural value of certain agricultural property.

Part 1
A Detailed Overview of the Inheritance Tax Regime

1.1 A reminder

The majority of people reading this book should acquaint themselves with this Part before reading the other sections of the book that deal with tax planning, etc. In particular, all readers should consider and understand the following before proceeding further:

- The Executive Overview of Inheritance Tax Regime (in the Introduction)
- IHT in a nutshell (transfers of value) (1.2)
- The nil-rate band and the rate of IHT (1.5)
- The spouse/civil partner exemption (1.8)
- The transferable nil-rate band (1.9)

Please bear in mind that reducing the burden of tax on your estate should be secondary to other objectives such as maintaining the lifestyle that you desire.

1.2 IHT in a nutshell (transfers of value)

Inheritance tax (often abbreviated to IHT) is essentially a wealth tax that is charged when wealth changes hands.

It is a tax that is charged principally on death. This is because the biggest transfer of wealth usually occurs on death. Inheritance tax may be charged during a person's lifetime, but the occasion when it is charged most often is on death.

The technical legal term for the tax is that it is a charge on a 'transfer of value'.

This begs the question of what is a 'transfer of value'?

A transfer of value is what happens when you dispose of something of value (e.g. money), and you are worth less than you were before you disposed of it.

A transfer of value has three ingredients:

1. There must be a transfer. A transfer means the passing of something, usually ownership rights, from an individual.
2. The transfer must be of value. Value means money or something of monetary or material worth. The transfer must therefore reduce the value of the estate of the transferor.
3. The transfer must be gratuitous. I.e. the person who makes the transfer must not have received money or any other benefit for it; and the person in receipt of the value must not have paid for it.

An easy way to understand the concept is that a transfer of value is what happens when you give away money, property or assets. You can give away some of your money, property and assets during your lifetime whenever you want, and you will inevitably give away all of your money, property and assets on death.*

*The transfer on death would not be a transfer of value were it not for a mechanism in the Inheritance Tax Act 1984 which artificially introduces a deemed transfer of value on death of everything a person owns: "On the death of any person tax shall be charged as if, immediately before his death, he had made a transfer of value and the value transferred by it had been equal to the value of his estate immediately before his death." (IHTA 1984 s4 (1))

Hence IHT can be charged while you are alive or on your death. However, as will be explained later, most gifts or "transfers of value" that you make during your lifetime are unlikely to be subject to inheritance tax.

Inheritance tax is charged on the value of the transfer – i.e. the amount by which the value of the transferor's estate is reduced.

Inheritance tax is not charged if you sell something to somebody else for the full market value, as there will have been no transfer of value between you and the purchaser. You and the purchaser will both own the same amount of value as you owned prior to the sale; but you will have exchanged an asset for the cash value and the purchaser will have exchanged his cash for the value of the asset.

Inheritance tax may be an issue if you buy an item for more than it is worth, as in those circumstances you will have transferred value to the vendor. (The difference between what the item is worth and what you have paid for it will amount to a transfer of value on your part.) However, you are unlikely to find that IHT is an issue merely because you have made a bad bargain with someone!

Although for most practical purposes a transfer of value can be thought of as being equivalent to a gift, or the transfer of wealth on death, it is important to be aware that transfers of value can include any or all of the following:

- all direct gifts of money, property or assets from one person to another
- all direct gifts of money, property or assets from one person to a trust
- all sales of property for less than the market value if the property was not sold on the open market (e.g. if a parent sold a house to his or her child at less than the full market value)
- granting a lease for less than the full market value
- re-arranging the shares in a private limited company
- agreeing to act as a guarantor for someone else's debts

- paying premiums on a policy of life assurance for somebody else's benefit
- failing to exercise a right you have and thereby reducing the value of your estate.

This list of transfers is not necessarily comprehensive. There may be other circumstances in which a transfer will take place.

The remainder of the book will often refer to "transfers of value", or simply to "transfers". If you find this confusing, you can refer to this section to refresh your memory on what a transfer consists of and what might be defined as a transfer.

Summary

Inheritance tax is a tax on the transfer of wealth on death and on transfers of wealth made within seven years of death. Technically these are known as "transfers of value" and include gifts and many other forms of transfer.

For most practical purposes, and for most people, a transfer of value will be either a gift or the transfer that takes place on death.

Two factors account for the reason that the tax is most commonly encountered on death:

1. the way that the tax is imposed (which is on transfers of value); and
2. the fact that death is the time that most people make their largest transfers of value – everything they possess.

1.3 The meaning of domicile

It may be important to have a basic grasp of the meaning of the word "domicile", as your domicile can have a bearing on how IHT will be charged on your money, property and assets.

"Domicile" is a word which refers to the country in which you have your permanent home, or are presumed to have your permanent home.

You will be domiciled in the UK if the following all apply:

- your parents are and always have been UK citizens
- they have (or had, if they have predeceased you) their permanent home in the UK
- you were dependent on them until you became an adult
- your parents always remained in the UK (other than for holidays!); and
- you were born in the UK and have lived here ever since.

Or if the following all apply:

- your parents were married prior to your birth
- your father is or was a UK citizen
- he had his permanent home in the UK
- you were dependent on him until you became an adult
- he always remained in the UK (other than for holidays!); and
- you were born in the UK and have lived here ever since.

Or if the following all apply:

- your parents were not married
- your mother is or was a UK citizen
- your mother had her permanent home in the UK
- you were dependent on her until you became an adult

- your mother always remained in the UK (other than for holidays!); and
- you were born in the UK and have lived here ever since.

If the above do not apply to you, then refer to 1.14.

Note about UK domicile

Strictly speaking, it is not possible to be domiciled in the UK. Your domicile may be in the legal jurisdiction of England and Wales, Scotland or Northern Ireland, but not the UK. However, in the interests of simplifying matters, we can consider the matter in terms of UK domicile. Even the Inheritance Tax Act 1984 does so (s18 IHTA 1984 uses the expression "... *domiciled* in the United Kingdom...")

1.4 The geographical ambit of IHT

'Ambit' simply means scope.

If an individual is domiciled in the UK, IHT is applied to all his money, property and assets wherever in the world they may be situated.

If an individual is not domiciled in the UK, but is nevertheless deemed to be domiciled in the UK by the operation of the law (i.e. under the criteria of 1.14), IHT is applied to all his money, property and assets wherever in the world they may be situated.

If an individual is not domiciled in the UK, IHT only applies to such of his money, property and assets that are located in the UK.

1.5 The nil-rate band and the rate of IHT

The easiest way to get to grips with inheritance tax is to consider what happens on death. If you read the executive summary earlier, some of this should be getting familiar to you now.

On a person's death, the first £325,000 of what he or she owns can be transferred to his or her heirs tax-free; this is known as the nil-rate band (often abbreviated to the NRB). Everything above the figure of £325,000 is taxed at the rate of 40%.

Example

If a George had money, property and assets (an 'estate') with a value of £425,000, and died in 2010, £325,000 would pass free of tax to his heirs; the remaining £100,000 would be taxed at the rate of 40%, giving rise to an inheritance tax charge of £40,000.

Note that inheritance tax is not just charged on the assets that are transferred on death. *It is also charged on assets that are transferred within seven years of the date of death. In exceptional circumstances* (explained in 1.15.5) *it may even be charged on assets transferred up to 14 years prior to the date of death.* The value of such gifts is added to the value of the assets held by the deceased at death, then the total value is subjected to inheritance tax. This is known as 'cumulation'.

Example

If George gave away the sum of £200,000 to his son Eric in 2009, then died in 2010 owning £425,000 which he left to his daughter in his will, the charge to inheritance tax on death would be based on a figure of £625,000 rather than £425,000, as follows:

	£
Value of George's Estate:	425,000
Add: gift to Eric:	200,000
Total:	625,000
Less: NRB:	(325,000)
Value to be taxed:	300,000

£300,000 @ 40% = £120,000.

Note that the nil-rate band has not always been £325,000 and it is unlikely to remain at £325,000 for long. It usually rises each year, roughly in rise with inflation.

At the time of writing, the NRB is £325,000.

In the tax year April 6 2008 to April 5 2009 it was £312,000.

In the tax year April 6 2009 to April 5 2010 it was £325,000.

In the tax year April 6 2010 to April 5 2011 it will remain at £325,000. (In fact it may remain at £325,000 until 2014.)

Appendix 1 provides details of nil-rate bands going back to 1914.

It is worth taking note of what the words 'nil-rate band' actually mean. The nil-rate band could have been called (for example) the 'tax-free band', or the 'exempt band', as this is what it appears to be. However, appearances may be deceptive. The nil-rate band is a band with a rate of tax at 0%. This perhaps leaves the door open for a future government to change it from the nil-rate band to (for example) 'the 5% rate band'.*

*The IHTA 1984 s7 states that: "the tax charged on the value transferred... shall be charged at the... rate or rates applicable to that value under the...Table in Schedule 1 to this Act..." The table in Schedule 1 refers to a rate of 0% and a rate of 40%.

Technical terms have been avoided in this book as far as possible, but nevertheless the remainder of the book will use a number of words you may not be accustomed to hearing. These are explained in the Glossary at the end of the book, but it is worth reminding you of the main ones you have encountered up to this point.

Estate	This refers to the money, property and assets that a person owns. It includes everything he possesses – shares, bank accounts, his house, etc.
NRB	The value of the money, property and assets that can be transferred (e.g. on death) at a rate of tax of 0%
Transfers of value or transfers	A transfer (in the context of IHT) means the passing of legal rights, usually ownership rights, from one person to another. Value in this context means money or material worth.

These concepts are explained in 1.2 'IHT in a nutshell'.

1.6 The ticking seven-year clock

You will observe from the examples in 1.5 that if you make a gift in the last seven years of your life, it can effectively reduce the nil-rate band available at your death. For example, if you make a gift of £325,000, and you die within a year, there will be no nil-rate band. Your entire estate will be taxed at 40%.

The activation of this reduction of the NRB will last for seven years after a gift is given, after which your nil-rate band will not be affected.

Example

George makes a gift of £200,000 cash in 2002. This reduces the nil-rate band available at his death by the figure of £200,000.

On the seventh anniversary of the gift, in 2009, his nil-rate band is restored to the full amount available.

1.7 Many nil-rate bands

Because of the seven-year clock referred to in 1.6, the nil-rate band could be considered as being available for use once every seven years, although we routinely consider it as available just once, on death.

Example

Sam is aged 50 in 2010. He decides to make a gift amounting to the full value of the nil-rate band on his 50th birthday, and every seven years after that until he is 71. By the age of 71, he will have made four gifts each amounting to his full nil-rate band. Assuming that the nil-rate band will remain at its current level of £325,000, he will have given away £1,300,000 tax-free by his 71st birthday.

When he dies aged 80, he still has the full nil-rate band available to offset against the value of his estate at death, because more than seven years have elapsed since the date of his last gift.

1.8 The spouse/civil partner exemption

We have seen how transfers of value are taxed at 0% up to the value of the nil-rate band (currently £325,000) and at 40% for transfers above that value.

Transfers of value between husband and wife, or civil partners (CP), are exempt from inheritance tax. This is known as the spouse/civil partner exemption.

Example

Gill dies leaving everything she owns to her husband Sam. Her estate is valued at £1,000,000. There is no inheritance tax payable on the estate, even though it exceeds the value of her nil-rate band of £325,000.

Since husbands and wives and civil partners often leave everything they own to one another, the effect of the spouse/civil partner exemption is that in most cases there is no inheritance tax payable on the death of the first spouse or a civil partner; it is only on the second death, as a rule, that inheritance tax will become an issue. How to deal with this point is covered in 1.9.

Planning issue

Transfers between spouses where one of them is not UK domiciled are only exempt to the extent that they do not exceed £55,000.

A UK domiciled spouse can only give his non-UK domiciled spouse a maximum of £55,000 free of IHT. And when this £55,000 spouse exemption has been used up, it is gone forever, unlike the nil-rate band. It will not be available again in seven years. Further transfers above and beyond the £55,000 spouse exemption limit from the UK domiciled spouse will be subject to IHT. However, the nil-rate band will be available in the usual way, to offset against the value of any such transfers.

By contrast, a non-UK domiciled spouse can give his UK domiciled spouse *any amount free of IHT*, thanks to the full spouse exemption.

1.9 The transferable nil-rate band

Because of the spouse/CP exemption (1.8), if a spouse or CP were to die leaving everything to his or her surviving spouse or CP, there would be no inheritance tax to pay.

However, IHT would be an issue on the death of the surviving spouse or CP.

When the surviving spouse or CP died, the first £325,000 of his or her estate would be tax-free due to the nil-rate band, and the remainder would be taxed at the rate of 40%, just like that of a person who died having been single throughout his or her life.

However, the possibility exists to make the situation more favourable.

Since 9 October 2007, it has been possible to transfer the nil-rate band of the first spouse or civil partner to die to the estate of the surviving spouse or civil partner when they die.

Note that the transferable nil-rate band cannot be used to mitigate IHT due on lifetime gifts made by the surviving spouse at the time that they are made. It can only be used to mitigate the tax due at the time of death.

It perhaps should be stressed that it is the nil-rate band, and only the nil-rate band, that can be transferred. The lifetime exemptions mentioned in the Executive Overview and detailed in 1.16.1 cannot be transferred between spouses.

Example

Joan dies in 2010. She has an estate valued at £550,000. The charge to inheritance tax is £90,000.

This is calculated as follows:

	£
Value of Joan's Estate:	550,000
Less: NRB	(325,000)
Estate taxed at 40%	225,000
£225,000 @ 40%	90,000

Joan was predeceased by her husband Phillip, who died in 2001. Joan's personal representatives can apply to HMRC Capital Taxes Office using the appropriate form (currently IHT 402) to transfer Phillip's nil-rate band forward for use against the value of her estate, and, if they do so, no inheritance tax will be payable.

	£
Value of Joan's Estate:	550,000
Less: 2 x NRB	(650,000)
Estate taxed at 40%	Nil

Planning issues

1. The nil-rate band can only be transferred where the death of the *second* spouse or civil partner to die occurred on or after 9 October 2007.
2. The *full* nil-rate band can only be transferred where the death of the *first* spouse or civil partner occurred after 13 March 1975.
3. There may be a *limited* amount of nil-rate band to transfer where the death of the *first* spouse or civil partner occurred between 21 March 1972 and 12 March 1975.
4. There will be *no* nil-rate band available to transfer where the death of the *first* spouse or CP occurred before 21 March 1972.
5. The above limitations on the transferability of the nil-rate band arise from the changes to the tax regime that have taken place over the years. Prior to 13 March 1975 the tax we now know as inheritance tax was called estate duty and under the estate duty regime there was no general exemption for transfers between spouses, with the result that the nil-rate band could be used up by a transfer from husband to wife and vice versa.
6. Strictly speaking, it is not the nil-rate band that can be transferred, but the unused portion of the nil-rate band. In most cases the full amount of the nil-rate band will be available for transfer (because everything was left to the spouse), but in some cases all or part of it may have been used up. (E.g. If Phillip had made gifts to someone other than his wife which used up his nil-rate band prior to his death.)

7. The unused portion of the nil-rate band of the first spouse or civil partner to die is taken as a percentage and applied to the nil-rate band prevailing at the date of death of the second spouse or civil partner to die. E.g. if the first death occurred in 2007, when the nil-rate band was £300,000, and the first spouse had used up half of this by giving some things away, the transferable nil-rate band on the second death (if that was in 2010) would not be 50% of £300,000, it would be 50% of £325,000 = £162,500.

8. The transferable nil-rate band is not transferred automatically. The transfer must be requested by the personal representatives of the surviving spouse or civil partner. Note: The personal representatives are the individuals who deal with the affairs of the deceased person on whose estate the tax is liable. If there is a will, the personal representatives will usually be the executors named in the will; if there is no will (i.e. if the deceased died intestate) the personal representatives will usually be the relatives entitled to the estate under the rules of intestacy. The personal representatives must apply to HMRC Capital Taxes Office in Nottingham to have the nil-rate band transferred, using the appropriate form, currently known as an IHT 402. They have two years from the date of death of the second spouse or civil partner in which to request the transfer of the unused portion of the nil-rate band of the first spouse or civil partner to pass away. If they miss this deadline, they will not be permitted to transfer the nil-rate band and the consequences could be disastrous. (E.g. in the case of Joan's estate, discussed above, missing the deadline would mean the avoidable

and unnecessary payment of £90,000 in IHT!) Note that what is transferred is the unused portion of the nil-rate band at the death of the first spouse to die. This unused portion cannot be restored to a full nil-rate band by the passage of time, no matter how long it is before the second spouse dies.

9. The transferable nil-rate band can only be used in respect of transfers on death, not lifetime transfers. To recap: if the surviving spouse makes lifetime gifts which are immediately chargeable to inheritance tax, the transferable nil-rate band cannot be used to mitigate the tax that is immediately payable. The transferable nil-rate band can only be transferred when the second spouse dies. It may then be used to mitigate all the tax payable on his estate, whether imposed in respect of his death estate or in respect of gifts made during his lifetime.
10. It is important to appreciate that the transferable nil-rate band is an *additional* nil-rate band which is *independent of* the nil-rate band of the surviving spouse.
11. The official form which is used to transfer the unused portion of the nil-rate band is currently known as the IHT 402.

1.10 Using up the transferable nil-rate band

The amount of nil-rate band available to transfer depends on the extent to which the spouse or civil partner who dies first has used up his or her nil-rate band by making transfers. These transfers could be made either as lifetime transfers in the seven years prior to their death (as we have seen, these would usually be gifts) or transfers on death.

The transfers on death could be made directly by the first spouse/CP in their will; or by the surviving spouse/CP in what are sometimes called "post death rearrangements".

> Post death rearrangements are arrangements which alter the way that an estate is distributed. For example, if you were given a sum of money by means of a gift from a will, you could make legal arrangements to have the sum of money given to your children instead of to you. If you made these arrangements in a certain legally compliant way, the gift of money to your children would be treated for tax purposes as if it had been made directly by the will to your children, rather than (as was really the case) by you. The legally compliant way would usually be by means of a document known as a deed of variation. This is all dealt with more fully at 3.2 and 3.3.

Transfers on death which reduce the value of the transferable nil-rate band are any dispositions of money, property or assets of any kind *which are given to anyone other than to an exempt beneficiary such as the surviving spouse or civil partner**.

Example

The nil-rate band was £200,000 in the tax year 1996-7. Syd died in July 1996, having made a lifetime gift of £50,000 in June of that year to his son Bert. On his death he therefore had 75% of his nil-rate band available.

In his will, Syd left a further £50,000 to Bert and the rest of his estate to his wife Rose.

The legacy of £50,000 to Bert used up a further 25% of Syd's nil-rate band. He then had 50% left.

---

*Exempt beneficiaries include charities and political parties. A gift to a charity or political party will not use up the nil-rate band (see 1.16).

Rose signed a deed of variation (this is a "post death rearrangement" as explained above) which varied the terms of Syd's will, giving yet another £50,000 to Bert. This used up another 25% of Syd's nil-rate band.

All told, Bert has received £150,000 from Syd's estate, which amounts to 75% of Syd's nil-rate band.

When Rose died in 2010, her executors could transfer the unused 25% of Syd's NEB to her estate. As the nil-rate band in 2010 was £325,000, there was £81,250 (25% x £325,000) available for them to transfer.

1.11 Multiple transferable nil-rate bands?

If an individual was married (or in a CP) and widowed, then married a second time, they would have an unused nil-rate band available from the death of their first spouse *and* potentially a further one available from his or her second spouse. You might think this would give them the possibility of having the advantage of three nil-rate bands – £325,000 x 3 (£975,000) free of tax. Sadly not.

Any one individual is only permitted to have the **value of one** *additional nil-rate band at death. However, this value may be accomplished through the use of more than one transferable nil-rate band. So an individual who has been widowed twice over may be able to take advantage of the transferable nil-rate bands of both his wives who have predeceased him in order to make up the value of one full transferable nil-rate band.*

The two nil-rate bands of the spouses who have predeceased can be used to make up the value of a single additional nil-rate band.

This means that if there is any surplus above and beyond the value of a single transferable nil-rate band, it may go to waste. (But note 1.12.3.)

Example

Paul was married to Kitty. Kitty died before Paul, with her full nil-rate band intact. If Paul died without remarrying, his executors would have his nil-rate band and that of Kitty to offset against the value of his estate.

If Paul remarried and survived his second wife, who also had a nil-rate band available, the total amount of nil-rate band available to Paul's executors would still only be two nil-rate bands (i.e. 2 x £325,000); Paul's nil-rate band and that of his second wife. The nil-rate band of Kitty cannot be used, as Paul's second wife's nil-rate band amounts to an *entire additional* nil-rate band.

If the nil-rate band of Kitty and Paul's second wife had been partially used up, then Paul's executors could have transferred both nil-rate bands to make up the value of one additional nil-rate band. However, if Paul had wholly or partially used up *his own* nil-rate band during his lifetime, his executors could not make up his nil-rate band to the full amount, even if there was an abundance of value available to transfer from the estates of Kitty and Paul's second wife which exceeded the value of a single transferable nil-rate band.

Example

If, when Kitty died, she had used up 75% of her nil-rate band, and Paul's second wife had used up 25% of her nil-rate band, Paul's executors would be entitled to claim the unused elements of both the nil-rate band of Kitty and of Paul's second wife to produce the value of one additional nil-rate band at Paul's death (75% + 25%.)

If Kitty had only used 50% of her nil-rate band, so that potentially there was 125% of the value of an additional nil-rate band available to transfer (Kitty's 50% + Paul's second wife's 75%) Paul's executors could still only claim the value of the one additional nil-rate band.

Conclusion

Although there may be more than one transferable nil-rate band, there can be no more than the value of one nil-rate band transferred. At times there may be less.

1.12 Maximising the tax savings from transferable nil-rate bands

1.12.1 Consequences of making gifts

There is an argument to the effect that making gifts can have an adverse effect on the transferable nil-rate band. A gift made in the seven years prior to death will reduce or exhaust the value of the nil-rate band that the donor has at death; and subsequently his or her estate will not benefit from the increase in value of the nil-rate band that normally takes place and which would then be transferred to their spouse.

Example

If an individual is a widow, widower or surviving civil partner, he or she will have available the nil-rate band of his or her predeceased spouse or civil partner, less any reductions of this owing to gifts made in the last seven years of their life or on passing away.

If the predeceased spouse or civil partner died in 2007, having made a gift of £150,000, the transferable nil-rate band available in 2010 would be £162,500 (even though only half, or £150,000, was left of it in 2007 – it is the proportion, carried forward to the present day's nil-rate band, that counts; see 1.9).

If this were added to the nil-rate band of the second member of the couple to die, it would allow for a total tax-free transfer of £637,500 from the estate of the couple. (The transferable nil-rate band of £162,500, plus the nil-rate band of the second to die of £325,000.)

If the gift had not been made, the tax-free transfer on the second death could have been £650,000. (A nil-rate band of £325,000 plus a transferable nil-rate band of £325,000.)

Summary

The impact on your nil-rate band is one of the factors that you might want to take into account when making gifts.

1.12.2 Survivorship clauses in wills

There is an argument that survivorship clauses should not be included in the wills of married couples and those in civil partnerships.

A survivorship clause in a will is one which typically says something along the lines of:

> *"I give all my property to my husband provided that he survives me for the period of thirty days."*

If a will contained this clause and the husband died just after an increase in the nil-rate band, but just prior to the expiry of the thirty-day survivorship period, the estate could suffer as the increase in the nil-rate band would not be applied to the transferable nil-rate band.

Example

Kimberley is in a CP with Bertha, who dies on 20 March 2008, when the nil-rate band is £312,000.

Bertha's will contains a clause which states:

> *"I give all my property to my civil partner Kimberley provided that she survives me for the period of thirty days."*

Kimberley dies 29 days later on 18 April 2009.

The nil-rate band was increased to £325,000 as of 6 April 2009.

Kimberley's estate has the benefit of a nil-rate band of £325,000 as she died after the nil-rate band had been increased. There is no nil-rate band to transfer as Kimberley did not survive for the required period of 30 days, after which all of Bertha's property would have passed to her. Instead, Bertha's estate is given to other beneficiaries and her estate has the nil-rate band prevailing at 5 April 2009 of only £312,000.

The tax-free transfer from both estates has been £637,000.

Consider the example of Bertha and Kimberley again, but this time with the survivorship provision in Bertha's will removed so that the clause leaving her estate to Kimberley simply stated:

> *"I give all my property to my civil partner Kimberley."*

If the will had been written like this, then when Bertha died on 20 March 2008, Kimberley would have inherited her estate. On Kimberley's death 29 days later, Bertha's nil-rate band could have been transferred to Kimberley's estate and it would have had the value prevailing after 5 April 2009, i.e. £325,000. Added to Kimberley's own nil-rate band, it would have allowed a total of £650,000 to be transferred tax-free from both estates.

The survivorship clause in this situation effectively caused the loss of £13,000 of nil-rate band, and an avoidable charge to tax of £5,200 (£13,000 x 40%).

Of course, wills should not be written in a certain way just for the tax consequences. The most important issue is ensuring that the beneficiaries benefit as the testator or testatrix intended. Any tax planning has to fit in with this requirement, not override it.

Summary

When making wills, consider them in the round with your advisor and consider carefully (amongst other matters) whether you wish to include survivorship clauses.

1.12.3 Bereaved spouses and civil partners in second marriages

If a party to a marriage or civil partner is bereaved then marries a second time, he or she should consider including a gift in his or her will to someone other than his or her (second) spouse or civil partner. This could potentially allow the couple to transfer £975,000 tax-free from their estates.

Example

Kieran is married to Paula. He is a widower who married a second time. Kieran and Paula have a son called Bada; neither have any other children.

Kieran dies in June 2009, leaving everything he owns to Paula. When Paula dies in 2010, leaving everything to Bada, her executors make use of her nil-rate band and Kieran's transferable nil-rate band to transfer £650,000 tax-free from her estate. (2 x £325,000.)

Supposing that Kieran made a will that was structured so as to leave a gift to the value of his nil-rate band to Bada, and everything else he owned to Paula, the outcome would have been more favourable.

On Kieran's death in June 2009, the nil-rate band was £325,000. This was the value of the gift that would have been made to Bada. Kieran would have had his nil-rate band (amounting to £325,000), but this need not have been used to make the gift to Bada tax free; instead, Kieran's executors could have transferred the nil-rate band from Kieran's first wife (assuming it had not been used up) to his estate to allow the gift to Bada to be made tax-free. The rest of Kieran's estate would have been given tax-free to Paula without making use of Kieran's NRB. (Due to the spouse exemption – 1.8.)

On Paula's death, as before, her executors would be able to make use of her nil-rate band and Kieran's transferable nil-rate band to transfer £650,000 tax-free from her estate. (2 x £325,000.)

As £325,000 would already have been transferred tax-free from Kieran's estate, that would make a total tax free transfer of £975,000.

Summary

If Kieran simply leaves his entire estate to Paula, the benefit of the nil-rate band of his first wife may be lost, as it cannot be claimed by Paula's executors. In order to maximise the tax savings available via nil-rate bands, Kieran must make a gift of the full available amount of his predeceased first wife's nil-rate band to someone other than Paula.

It should, perhaps, be added that this is only applicable if he predeceases Paula, unless Paula makes a gift amounting to the value of her own nil-rate band to Bada on her death, rather than to Kieran. Kieran's estate cannot benefit from the value of more than one transferable nil-rate band, so if he is predeceased by Paula and she leaves everything to him, then on his death only £650,000 can be given tax-free to Bada. But if Paula predeceases Kieran and gives £325,000 to Bada in her will, this leaves the door open to Kieran's executors to transfer the nil-rate band of his first wife for use against the tax liability of his estate and give an additional £650,000 tax free to Bada.*

*This example illustrates the principles involved with transferable NRBs, where one of the spouses is in a second marriage and has the benefit of a transferable NRB from a prior marriage. In practice, many couples may not be sufficiently wealthy to give away a full NRB on the first death. In such cases it may be preferable for both spouses to give the value of a NRB into a discretionary trust (see 1.24) on the first death. This could give either spouse access to funds from the trust if necessary. (Similar to the scheme outlined in 2.12 – but with greater tax benefits.) In the unlikely event that both spouses have the benefit of a transferable NRB from a prior marriage, it may be advisable for both spouses to direct the value of two NRBs into a discretionary trust on the first death. Pilot trusts may be preferable for this purpose (see 2.22).

1.13 Evidential issues raised by transferable nil-rate bands

As noted above, the amount of nil-rate band available to transfer depends on the extent to which the spouse or civil partner who dies first has used up his or her nil-rate band by making transfers; and the extent to which post death rearrangements have eroded the nil-rate band of the predeceased spouse or civil partner.

This can create problems for executors seeking to transfer a nil-rate band. How do they know whether the spouse who predeceased made any transfers at all, particularly if he or she died many years ago? How do they know what (if any) post death rearrangements were entered into by the surviving spouse?

There are records that can be checked, but at best these may provide only partial answers.

The lack of hard information might not be too much of a problem if the spouse or civil partner who predeceased died prior to 9 October 2007. Since the legislation that introduced transferable nil-rate bands only came into force on that date, those individuals who died without ever being aware of the transferable nil-rate band could not be expected to maintain records to assist the executors of the estates of their deceased spouses many years down the line.

It appears that HMRC accepts this and that all that can be expected of personal representatives is that they should make all reasonable enquiries prior to claiming a transferable nil-rate band.

The situation may be different for estates where the date of death of the first spouse to die was on or after 9 October 2007. It may be that these cases will be scrutinised more closely by HMRC, as it will be expected that there will be a general awareness of the transferable nil-rate band and of the corresponding need to retain records for the benefit of future executors.

1.14 More on domicile

Domicile is a concept which potentially raises very difficult issues. The best that can be done here is to acquaint you with some basic principles so that you are less likely to be caught out by it than would otherwise be the case.

Every individual has a domicile; it is not possible to have more than one domicile.

There are three types of domicile in UK law: domicile of origin, domicile of choice and deemed domicile. Until you are an adult, there is also a fourth variety of domicile: domicile of dependency.

Domicile of origin

Everyone acquires a domicile of origin at birth. A legitimate child normally has the domicile of origin of his or her father; an illegitimate child normally has the domicile of origin of his or her mother.

Domicile of choice

A domicile of origin can be changed to a domicile of choice if you reside in a country with the intention of living permanently there.

There are many factors that must be taken into account to determine whether someone has a domicile of choice.

A domicile of choice can often be difficult to prove one way or the other.

Deemed domicile

A person who is not actually domiciled in the UK may nevertheless be deemed to be domiciled in the UK for the purposes of IHT at any time (known as "the relevant time") if:

- he was domiciled in the UK within the three years immediately preceding the relevant time, or
- he was resident (for income tax purposes) in the UK in not less than 17 of the 20 years of assessment for income tax, ending with the year of assessment for income tax in which the relevant time falls. The time period of 17 out of 20 years has no particular logic to it; it is simply a figure devised by the persons responsible for drafting the inheritance tax legislation.*

Domicile of dependency

If you are a minor and you are dependent on someone, your domicile may be the same as the domicile of the person on whom you are dependent. When you become an adult, you will be able to change your domicile to a domicile of choice.

Summary

In all but the most straightforward of cases, if there are issues concerning your domicile, you should consult a specialist text and possibly seek specialist advice.

1.15 The IHT charge on gifts (PETs and chargeable transfers)

1.15.1 Potentially exempt transfers (PETs)

While most significant transfers of value are made on death, transfers of value (including major transfers) can be made during an individual's lifetime. One of the most common forms that a

*IHTA 1984 s267

lifetime transfer of value can take is a straightforward gift from one individual to another.

Such a gift is known as a potentially exempt transfer, or a PET.

The name 'potentially exempt transfer' indicates that it is a transfer of value that is *potentially* exempt from inheritance tax at the time that it is made – but that it is necessary to wait (for seven years) and see whether it *actually* becomes exempt from inheritance tax. If the person who gives the gift does not die within those seven years, it is exempt.

Example

John, a very wealthy man, gives his son Henry £500,000. This is a PET.

If John makes the PET seven years or more prior to his death, it will be exempt from inheritance tax.

Example

John gives the £500,000 to Henry in 2002 and dies in 2010. The £500,000 is therefore exempt from inheritance tax because it has been gifted more than seven years prior to John's death.

The same gift made within seven years of the death of the person making it would be subject to inheritance tax. Sometimes this is referred to as a 'failed PET'.

Example

John gives Henry a further £500,000 in 2009, then dies in 2010. This gift will be subject to inheritance tax when John dies, at the rate of tax applicable on John's death. The £500,000 will be added to the value of John's estate for the purposes of calculating the inheritance tax due on his death. (However, his NRB will be deducted from the total in calculating the amount of tax that may be due). It has become a failed PET.

	£
Value of PET	500,000
Less: nil-rate band in 2010	325,000
Taxable portion of PET	175,000
Value of John's estate at death	500,000
Total	675,000
Tax at 40%	270,000
(Made up of tax on PET:	£70,000 (40% of £175,000)
And tax on estate:	£200,000 (40% of £500,000)

Note the following points:

- The transferee is liable to pay the tax on the failed PET (but note the comments later at 1.15.8).
- If HMRC fail to collect the tax from the transferee, liability for payment will fall on the executors, who will be obliged to pay the tax from the estate. This could potentially make personal representatives personally liable to pay the tax if a failed PET comes to light after they have distributed the estate.
- It could also be argued that the liability should trigger the grossing-up provisions (as outlined below at 1.15.4); however, the HMRC view appears to be that grossing up should not apply in these cases. The *Inheritance Tax Manual* used by tax inspectors is available for scrutiny on the internet at **www.hmrc.gov.uk**. It states at IHTM 30044 that in these circumstances "there is no question of grossing up the lifetime transfer."
- Somewhat worryingly, if personal representatives distribute an estate, then subsequently a failed PET comes to light, they could again find themselves personally liable to pay the tax on the failed PET. HMRC has stated on this issue that "we will not actually pursue for inheritance tax personal representatives

who after making the fullest enquiries that are reasonably practicable in the circumstances to discover lifetime transfers, and so having done all in their power to make full disclosure of them to the Board of HMRC have obtained a certificate of discharge and distributed the estate before a chargeable lifetime transfer comes to light." (Quoted in IHTM 30044.)

1.15.2 Transfers that are PETs

In order to qualify as a PET, a gift must reduce the value of the estate of the person who makes the transfer and increase the value of the estate of the person who receives the transfer. (A payment to a third party to confer some form of benefit – e.g. the payment of a private medical bill for another person – would not therefore qualify as a PET)*.

Subject to that requirement, the following are PETs:

- gifts made during the lifetime of an individual to another individual
- transfers to the trustees of a trust for the disabled (sees section 1.24)
- transfers made on the termination of a type of trust (see section 1.24) known as an IPDI trust (immediate post-death interest trust), where the trust assets are transferred to another special type of trust – a trust for bereaved minors. (However, transfers from an IPDI trust to the trustees of trusts other than bereaved minors' trusts are chargeable transfers – see sections 1.15.4 and 1.24.)

*Note that the payment of school fees for grandchildren (and many similar transactions) cannot be PETs – although such payments reduce the value of the estate of the transferor, they do not increase the value of the estate of the transferees. Such transfers may be covered by exemptions – e.g., the exemption for regular payments out of income (1.16.1.3) or maintenance of the family (1.16.1.4). If such a payment is not covered by one of the exemptions, it is likely to be chargeable. However, in most cases such a payment would probably fall within the transferor's nil-rate band.

1.15.3 Taper relief

The rate of tax payable on a failed PET is reduced by taper relief, a reduction that increases depending on the length of time that has passed from the time the failed PET was made to the death of the person who made it. The taper relief is applied against the tax payable on the PET as follows:

No. of years PET was made prior to death	Tax on PET is charged at this % of applicable rate on death
Between 3 and 4 years	80%
Between 4 and 5 years	60%
Between 5 and 6 years	40%
Between 6 and 7 years	20%

Summary

- A PET is not chargeable when it is first made.
- It is not chargeable if the donor survives the PET by seven years.
- It becomes chargeable if the donor dies within seven years of making the PET.
- Taper relief may be available to reduce the amount of tax that is charged.
- For a transfer to qualify as a PET, it must reduce the estate of the transferor and increase the estate of the transferee, otherwise it is likely to be chargeable (unless covered by an exemption – see above).

Common misconception

It appears to be a common misconception that taper relief is applied to the PET itself, so that a PET of £500,000 made four years ago would be reduced by 80% for tax purposes and treated as a PET of £100,000. This is not the case. It is the *rate of tax payable on the PET* which is subject to taper relief.

This means that taper relief does not confer any benefit where the transfer is within the nil-rate band. Taper relief reduces the rate of tax charged. If the rate of tax is nil, there can logically be no reduction in it.

Example

If a transferor makes a PET of £425,000, this may be subject to an IHT charge.

However, because the PET is *potentially* exempt, the IHT will not be charged unless the transferor dies within seven years of making the PET. If he dies more than three years after making the PET (but, of course, within seven years of making it), taper relief will be available (on the *tax due* on the PET at the date of death).

A PET of £200,000 is not subject to tax, as it falls within the transferor's nil-rate band (as would any gift up to the current rate of the nil-rate band). Consequently if the transferor dies, say, five years after making a PET amounting to the value of his nil-rate band or less, no taper relief will be available.

Planning issue

If you are planning to mitigate the impact of inheritance tax by using PETs, it is clearly a good idea to do so when you are in good health and have reasonable prospects of surviving the PET by seven years or more.

1.15.4 Chargeable transfers

Chargeable transfers are those transfers that are made by a person during his lifetime and that are immediately chargeable to inheritance tax – in other words, there is a charge to tax *at the time that the gift is made*. Generally speaking, these will be transfers into trusts.*

At this point you may be wondering what a trust might be. It is beyond the scope of this book to fully explain trusts; however, 1.24 provides a brief explanation and should be adequate to enable you to understand the distinction between making a gift to an individual (which is a PET) and making a gift to a trust (which is usually a chargeable transfer).

While most transfers into trusts are chargeable transfers, some transfers into trusts are treated as PETs. Those trusts into which a transfer will be a PET rather than a chargeable transfer are trusts in which there is a qualifying disabled person's interest and those which are transitional serial interests. It is beyond the scope of this book to explain such trusts in any depth and you are recommended to always take professional advice when dealing with trusts.

Lifetime chargeable transfers are taxed, when they are made, at half the rate of inheritance tax applicable on death (i.e. 20% as opposed to 40%). This 20% is not charged on the entire amount of the chargeable transfer; it is only charged on the amount of the transfer that exceeds the nil-rate band. (Or available nil-rate band.)

Where a lifetime chargeable transfer was made after April 5 and prior to October 1 in any year, this 20% tax is due on the 30 April in the following year; where the transfer was made after 30 September and prior to 6 April in any year, the 20% tax is due six months after the end of the month in which the transfer was made.

*Under S3A IHTA only the transfers referred to in 1.15.2 can be PETs; this means that most other transfers, including e.g. transfers to limited companies, are chargeable. (Unless covered by one or other of the exemptions or reliefs referred to in 1.16 and 1.17.)

If the transferor dies within seven years of making a chargeable transfer, the transfer is added to his estate and the tax on the transfer is recalculated at the death rate. However, credit is given for the tax already paid. In addition, taper relief is given, as with PETs. The taper relief is as per the table in 1.15.3. If this is beginning to sound horribly complicated, hopefully the examples below will clarify matters.

Example 1

George pays the sum of £625,000 into a discretionary trust for his grandchildren in June 2008. He has made no other transfers within the previous seven years. The tax immediately payable on the transfer is calculated as follows:

	£
Chargeable transfer	625,000
Less: nil-rate band in June 2008	312,000
	313,000
Tax at 20% (half the death rate) =	62,600

George dies two years later in June 2010. The tax is recalculated by reference to the death rate:

	£
Chargeable transfer	625,000
Less: nil-rate band in June 2010	325,000
	300,000
Tax at 40% =	120,000
(Less: tax already paid at lifetime rate	62,200)
Additional tax payable on transfer on death =	57,400

Example 2

George pays the sum of £625,000 into a discretionary trust for his grandchildren in June 2005. He has made no other transfers within the previous seven years. The tax immediately payable on the transfer is calculated as follows:

	£
Chargeable transfer	625,000
Less: nil-rate band in June 2005	275,000
	350,000
Tax at 20% (half the death rate) =	70,000

George dies four years and eleven months later in May 2010. The tax is recalculated by reference to the death rate:

	£
Chargeable transfer	625,000
Less: nil-rate band in May 2010	325,000
	300,000
Tax at 40% =	120,000

However, as the transfer took place between four and five years prior to George's death, taper relief applies:

	£
£120,000 x 60%	72,000
Less: tax already paid	70,000
Additional tax due =	2,000

Example 3

George pays the sum of £625,000 into a discretionary trust for his grandchildren in June 2004. He has made no other transfers within the previous seven years. The tax immediately payable on the transfer is calculated as follows:

	£
Chargeable transfer	625,000
Less: nil-rate band June 2005	263,000
	362,000
Tax at 20% (half the death rate) =	72,400

George dies five years and eleven months later in May 2010. The tax is recalculated by reference to the death rate:

	£
Chargeable transfer	625,000
Less: nil-rate band in May 2010	325,000
	300,000
Tax at 40% =	120,000

However, as the transfer took place between four and five years prior to George's death, taper relief applies:

	£
£120,000 x 40% =	48,000

As the recalculated tax of £48,000 at the death rate is less than the tax already paid of £72,400, no further tax is payable. However, no refund is due!

Example 4

George pays the sum of £200,000 into a trust for his grandchildren. As this sum is less than the nil-rate band, there is no inheritance tax to pay immediately. If he survives for seven years after making the gift, there will, furthermore, be no tax resulting from it at the date of his death.

Grossing up

The person liable to pay the tax on a chargeable transfer is the transferor. This can lead to some unfortunate consequences known as 'grossing up'.

You will recall that IHT has to be paid on the amount by which the value of the transferor's estate is reduced. Because the transferor is liable for the tax on a lifetime chargeable transfer as well as the transfer itself, his estate is reduced by the value of the transfer PLUS the value of the tax payable on the transfer.

It is almost as if the transferor is expected to pay tax on his tax!

The result is that the amount of tax payable on the transfer is rather more than might be initially expected.

To ascertain the tax payable on the transfer, the transfer has to be grossed up to include the tax payable on it. Tax is then imposed on the grossed up value.

E.g. Assume that a transferor wishes to give £100,000 free of tax to his son. In addition, assume that all of his exemptions have been used up, and there are no reliefs that can be applied.

In order to give the sum of £100,000 tax-free, the donor must start with a gift of £125,000, which, subject to tax at 20%, will achieve a taxed figure of £100,000, since 20% of £125,000 is £25,000.

Turning this calculation around, to arrive at the tax-free figure for any immediately chargeable lifetime gift, you must start with the tax-free figure that you want, then gross it up by 5/4. You will note in the foregoing example that £125,000 is 5/4 of £100,000.

Example

Sam makes a payment of £525,000 into a discretionary trust. It might appear that the tax payable on this is £40,000. (£525,000 - £325,000 = £200,000; £200,000 @ 20% = £40,000.)

But the tax is more than £40,000, because it has to be calculated as follows:

	£
Chargeable amount:	200,000
Multiplied by the gross-up factor of 5/4 =	250,000
£250,000 taxed at lifetime rate of 20%:	£50,000

In other words, the tax is £10,000 more than might be expected because of grossing up.

If the tax is recovered from the transferee, though, grossing up does not apply; the transferor's estate is not reduced by the tax, and therefore they are not (as it were) taxed on that tax again.

The moral of this story would appear to be that prior to any chargeable transfer being made, there should be a written agreement between transferor and transferee stating that the transferee will be liable for paying the tax on the transfer, which the transferee should adhere to.

Taper relief

As with PETs, taper relief is applied to the tax payable on chargeable transfers and can reduce the balance payable on the death of the donor. To reiterate, it is applied using the same table given above at 1.15.3.

Summary

- A chargeable transfer is immediately chargeable to inheritance tax.
- The transferor is liable to pay the tax unless there is an agreement that the recipient pays the tax.
- If the chargeable transfer amounts to less than the nil-rate band prevailing at the date it is made, no IHT is payable. (Unless a subsequent chargeable transfer or failed PET brings it into the reckoning – see 1.15.6.)
- If it amounts to more than the nil-rate band, IHT is payable at the rate of 20% on the excess.
- If the donor survives the chargeable transfer by seven years, no further IHT is payable.
- If the donor dies within seven years there may be IHT (or additional IHT) to pay on the chargeable transfer, which may be reduced by taper relief (as shown in the examples given above in this section).

Planning issue

If you make a chargeable transfer you will be principally liable to pay the tax on it and this will result in grossing up. Therefore, if possible, there should be an agreement that the tax should be paid by the transferee.

Be wary of making a chargeable transfer that amounts to more than your nil-rate band, and, if you do, think very carefully about it and take advice.

If you make a chargeable transfer more than seven years prior to death, it may be subject to inheritance tax when it is made, but it will not be subject to further inheritance tax on death. (Unless it is brought into the reckoning by a later chargeable transfer or a failed PET – see below at 1.15.6).

1.15.5 Cumulation

When calculating the charge to tax on a chargeable transfer at the date it is made, the transfer must be added to all chargeable transfers made in the previous seven years in order to ascertain the tax due. This is known as cumulation.

Example

George makes a chargeable transfer of £200,000 in May 2007. He has made no previous chargeable transfers. There is no tax to pay because it falls within his nil-rate band, which at the time is £300,000.

George makes a further chargeable transfer of £200,000 in May 2010. This is within seven years of the earlier chargeable transfer.

This means that although the second transfer amounts to less than George's nil-rate band, there is still IHT to pay on it:

	£
May 2007 transfer	200,000
May 2010 transfer	200,000
TOTAL	400,000
Less: nil-rate band in 2010	325,000
Chargeable amount =	75,000
Tax due at 20% =	15,000

(And if cumulation applies, as per 1.15.4 the tax payable will be £18,750, i.e. 20% of the grossed-up figure of £93,750.)

Note that PETs are **not** cumulated with chargeable transfers, for the purposes of determining the charge to tax at the date that chargeable transfers are made.

Cumulation also applies to the death estate.

The transfers made in the seven years before death (lifetime chargeable transfers and failed PETs) are added to the death estate for tax purposes.

Example

Syd makes the following transfers:

- £100,000 to his son in February 2000
- £200,000 to his daughter in March 2008
- £200,000 to his son in July 2010.

Syd dies in September 2010 with an estate of £300,000.

The cumulable value on his death for tax is:

	£
March 2008	200,000
July 2010	200,000
September 2010	300,000
TOTAL	700,000

(The gift of February 2000 is outside seven years of the death and is omitted.)

Note that failed PETs *are* cumulated with chargeable transfers, for the purposes of determining the charge to tax at the *date of death*.

1.15.6 Adverse consequences of chargeable transfers and failed PETs – the 14-year rule

In calculating the IHT due on any transfer made within seven years of death, all chargeable transfers made in the seven years prior to that transfer must be taken into account, as noted in 1.15.6.

Similarly, if an individual makes a PET then dies within seven years of the PET so that it becomes chargeable, the PET will have the consequence that any chargeable transfer made within the seven years prior to the PET will also become chargeable.

Both these things mean that inheritance tax can be charged on gifts made up to *14 years* prior to the date of death of the donor/transferor.

Example

Syd makes the following transfers:

- £200,000 to a discretionary trust in April 1998
- £100,000 to his daughter in July 2001
- £100,000 to his son in February 2004

- £200,000 to his daughter in March 2008
- £200,000 to his son in July 2010.

Syd dies in September 2010 with an estate of £300,000.

The cumulable value on his death for tax is:

[illegible]	£
April 1998	200,000
February 2004	100,000
March 2008	200,000
July 2010	200,000
September 2010	300,000
TOTAL	1,000,000

The gift in April 1998 of £200,000 has been dragged into the calculation even though it was made more than seven years prior to Syd's death. It has been drawn in by the failed PET made in February 2004.

The PET made to Syd's daughter in July 2001 is omitted from the reckoning as it was made more than seven years prior to the date of death; it is a successful PET.

Summary

If a person dies within seven years of making a PET or chargeable transfer, all chargeable transfers made within the seven years prior to the PET or chargeable transfer will be brought within the charge to tax on death.

1.15.7 Liability for payment of tax on PETs

The law states that if a transferor dies within seven years of making a PET, the person who is primarily liable to pay the tax on the PET is the transferee (i.e., the person who has received it).

This might suggest that in all cases where there has been a PET, and the transferor dies within seven years of making it, triggering a charge to inheritance tax, the transferee will be liable to pay the tax.

It is, however, not quite as straightforward as that. The transferee will only be liable to pay the tax on a PET if the PET becomes *chargeable in its own right.*

Unfortunately, this is a concept that can probably only be properly explained by means of worked examples.

Before you read through the examples, you will need to be aware of how IHT is apportioned between the recipients of any PETs, and the executors who are responsible for administering the estate at death.

What happens is that PETs are cumulated with the death estate (as explained in 1.15.6). The nil-rate band at the value it was at the date of death is then applied to the PETs in the order that they were made. To the extent that they fall within the value of the nil-rate band, the PETs will not be subject to IHT, and the transferees will not have to pay anything. Any PET that exceeds the nil-rate band will be *chargeable in its own right* and the transferee will have to pay the inheritance tax due on it.

Example 1

This is the example used in 1.15.1.

John gives Henry £500,000 in 2009, then dies in 2010. This gift will be will be subject to inheritance tax when John dies, at the rate of tax applicable on John's death. The £500,000 will be added to the value of John's estate for the purposes of calculating the inheritance tax due on his death. (However, his nil-rate band will be deducted from the total in calculating the amount of tax that may be due.) It has become a failed PET.

	£
Value of PET	500,000
Less: nil-rate band in 2010	325,000
Taxable portion of PET	175,000
Value of John's estate at death	500,000
Total	675,000
Tax at 40%	270,000
(Made up of tax on PET:	£70,000 (40% of £175,000)
And tax on estate:	£200,000 (40% of £500,000)

In this example, the PET exceeds the NRB and is chargeable in its own right, so the transferee has to pay the IHT due on it. The executors must pay the IHT due on the death estate from the estate assets.

Example 2

This is a variation on the example used in 1.15.1.

Supposing that instead of giving Henry £500,000 in 2009, John gave him only £300,000, then died in 2010. The result would be to increase the IHT payable on John's estate on death. This gift will be subject to inheritance tax when John dies, at the rate of tax applicable on John's death. However, the liability for paying all the IHT would fall on John's executors, as the PET would not be chargeable in its own right.

	£
Value of PET	300,000
Value of John's estate at death	500,000
Total	800,000
Less: NRB in 2010:	325,000
Taxable amount:	475,000
Tax at 40%	190,000

(However, the NRB is applied to the PET in priority to the estate. As the PET is less than the NRB, it is not chargeable in its own right, and there is no tax to pay on it. The executors pay the entire tax bill of £190,000. Although the existence of the PET has brought about a higher charge to tax on the death estate, the transferee is not liable to pay the tax on this occasion.)

Example 3

This is another variation on the example used in 1.15.1, to illustrate what happens when there are many PETs.

Supposing that John gave £200,000 to Peter in 2008, and £200,000 to John in 2009, then died in 2010:

	£
Value of PET given to Peter:	200,000
Value of PET given to John:	200,000
Value of John's estate at death	500,000
Total	900,000
Less: NRB in 2010:	325,000
Taxable amount:	575,000
Tax at 40%	230,000

The NRB is applied first to the PET given to Peter, as that was the earliest PET. As his PET fell within the NRB, Peter does not have to pay any of the IHT.

However, Peter's PET used up £200,000 of the NRB. This means that only £125,000 is available to apply against John's PET, so John's PET has become chargeable in its own right, and he must bear the burden of tax on it:

	£
John's PET:	200,000
Less: remaining NRB	125,000
Taxable amount:	75,000
Tax at 40%	30,000 (payable by John)

The £200,000 burden of tax on the death estate is a liability of the executors that is payable from the estate.

Note that if the PETs had been made on the same day, each PET would benefit from a proportion of the nil-rate band, and that Peter and John would bear the burden of the IHT on a pro-rata basis. (Which would mean that they would pay equal amounts in this example.)

1.15.8 If you intend to make both PETs and chargeable transfers, which should you make first?

This is a question to which there is probably no hard-and-fast rule. Each case must be considered on its own merits, and the consequences of making one kind of transfer prior to another must be thought through.

Some of the issues are as follows:

1. When PETs and chargeable transfers are made in the same financial year, the annual exemption (see 1.16.1.1) of £3,000 is applied against earlier transfers in priority to later transfers. So if a PET is made prior to a chargeable transfer, this could deprive the chargeable transfer of the benefit of the annual exemption, and result in a larger charge to IHT than would have been the case if the chargeable transfer had been made before the PET.

2. There are points relating to relevant property trusts that may need to be taken into account. (An explanation of relevant

property trusts is given at 1.24.) Most new trusts will be relevant property trusts. Relevant property trusts are subject to various IHT charges. If a PET is made prior to a chargeable transfer into a trust, and the PET subsequently becomes chargeable, this will have the consequence that the trust will pay more tax than would have been the case had the PET been made after the chargeable transfer. If a transferor dies more than three years but less than seven years after making his PET and chargeable transfer, the fact that the PET preceded the chargeable transfer could result in less IHT being payable on the transfers themselves than would have been the case if the chargeable transfer had preceded the PET.

3. There is a case to be made that where an individual has a history of making both chargeable lifetime transfers and PETs, his PETs should be made first, with a substantial lapse of time between them and the chargeable transfers. (So as to maximise the chances of the PETs falling out of the reckoning at the date of death.)

4. Where there is a history of making chargeable transfers, and there are plans to make a PET, consideration should be given about the consequences of the PET becoming chargeable and dragging all the previous chargeable transfers into the reckoning at the date of death.

1.16 Exemptions (transfers that are exempt from IHT)

Some transactions are exempt from inheritance tax. The range of exempt transactions is wide and confusing.

Some exemptions apply only to lifetime transfers, some apply only to the deemed transfer on death, and some apply to both lifetime transfers and the deemed transfer on death.

The main exemptions are as follows.

1.16.1 Lifetime exemptions

This covers those exemptions that only apply to lifetime transfers (e.g. gifts made by you while you are alive rather than by your will). Taxation will only apply to money which exceeds the levels set by these exemptions, if the giver dies within seven years of making the gifts or payments. In some cases this may be 14 years – see 1.15.4.

The exemption is not on the sum forever; nor for both giver and receiver: *it is on the sum as given by the giver*. Naturally, money received as a gift can, eventually, form part of the receiver's estate on their death, along with all their money and property, and will effectively be taxed at that point should it be part of an estate that exceeds the nil-rate band.

1.16.1.1 The annual £3,000 exemption

You may give away up to £3,000 in any one year to any individual you like and it will be exempt from inheritance tax.

If the £3,000 is not used it may be rolled forward to the next year – but not further than that. So you may have (at most) £6,000 of annual exemption available to use in any one year.

If you have the £3,000 exemption available one year and you make a gift of, say, £5,000, then the first £3,000 in value of the gift will be exempt due to the annual exemption.

1.16.1.2 Small gifts of £250 or less

Small gifts (£250 or less in any one tax year) are exempt from inheritance tax. You may therefore make as many gifts as you like during the tax year, so long as the gifts amount to £250 *each* or less, and are given to *different individuals*.

This is obviously of limited value unless you have, say, a large number of grandchildren and nephews and nieces on whom you wish to confer a modest benefit.

You cannot make a gift of £500 and expect the first £250 to be exempt due to the small gift allowance; if you make a gift above the £250 figure, the *entire* gift becomes taxable if you die within seven years of giving it, not just the extent to which it exceeds £250.

Nor can you mix and match the £3,000 annual exemption with the small gift allowance. If you make a gift of £3,250 to an individual, the £250 will not be exempt. This exemption cannot be used in conjunction with the annual exemption, so it is not possible to make a gift totalling £3,250 to an individual in any one tax year, and claim that this is tax free because the annual exemption covers the first £3,000 and the small gifts exemption covers the remaining balance of £250.

1.16.1.3 Regular payments out of income

If you make regular payments out of income, these are exempt from inheritance tax when you die. They must be:

- within your normal expenditure
- made out of your income
- and after allowing for all transfers of value forming part of your normal expenditure, they must leave you with sufficient income to maintain your usual standard of living.

1.16.1.4 Maintenance of the family

Gifts which are made during life for the purpose of maintaining your children are exempt provided the child is under 18 or undergoing full-time education. This exemption also covers step-children and adopted children. A separate provision provides the exemption in respect of illegitimate children.

Similarly, lifetime gifts which are made for the care or maintenance of a dependant relative are exempt from inheritance tax. The care or maintenance must be the kind which it is 'reasonable' to provide; and the dependant relative must be either:

(a) your mother or father, or your spouse's or civil partner's mother or father; or

(b) a relative of you or of your spouse or civil partner, who is incapacitated by old age or infirmity from maintaining themselves.

Note that the expression 'reasonable' is not defined in the legislation (IHTA 1984 s11(3), but HMRC have in their *Inheritance Tax Manual* stated (at IHTM04177) that "'Reasonable' would appear to suggest such amount as is reasonably necessary for the purpose of providing care and maintenance (but no more)."

1.16.1.5 Gifts in consideration of marriage/civil partnership

This exemption seems on the face of it straightforward, but on closer inspection is surprisingly complex.

Parents

If you are a parent of someone who is getting married or entering a civil partnership, you may make a gift of up to £5,000 to either party (but not to both parties) to the marriage or civil partnership and it will be exempt from inheritance tax. The child of yours who is entering into the marriage or civil partnership can include an illegitimate child, adopted child, or stepchild.

However, note that:

- the gift must be made on the occasion of the marriage or civil partnership (it can be shortly before the actual event)
- it must be conditional on the marriage or civil partnership taking place, and

- it must be made by you for the purpose of, or with a view to encouraging or facilitating, the marriage or civil partnership.

These three conditions apply to all the other classes of gifts in consideration of marriage which follow below.

Party to the marriage or civil partnership

Either party to the marriage can make a gift in consideration of marriage to the other party of up to £2,500, which will be exempt from IHT.

Remoter ancestors

A remoter ancestor than a parent can make an outright gift of up to £2,500 to either party to the marriage, which will be exempt from IHT.

Other persons

Any other person can make an outright gift of up to £1,000 to either party to the marriage, which will be exempt from IHT.

These are the rules which apply to outright gifts. It is possible to make exempt gifts into trusts for the benefit of the couple who are getting married or entering into a civil partnership, with the financial limits as set out above. It is unlikely that it would be worthwhile setting up a trust with such a modest amount of money. The full rules relating to how such a trust should be set up to qualify for the exemption are somewhat complex, and if you are interested in exploring them I can only refer you to an appropriate advisor or to the Inheritance Tax Act 1984 s22. I would caution you that the cost of setting up such a trust might in some cases exceed the value of the exemption!

1.16.1.6 Transactions not intended to confer a gratuitous benefit

If you buy a car for more than it is worth, you will have transferred value to the car salesman (as most of us do!) but it will not be a transfer of value that could attract a charge to IHT. Transfers of value are only subject to IHT if they are intended to confer a *gratuitous benefit** (i.e. you have to intend that the benefit should be enjoyed without delivery of a service, product or payment to you).

This is known as the purchase exemption. It means that normal commercial transactions do not trigger a charge to IHT. Hence the comments in 1.2 regarding making a bad bargain.

1.16.2 Transfers that are exempt transfers whether lifetime or death transfers

The following transfers are exempt whether the transfer is a lifetime transfer or a transfer on death.

The nil-rate band

As previously mentioned, transfers up to the value of the nil-rate band are taxed at 0% and to all intents and purposes this means they are (for the time being at least!) exempt transfers. This is the case whether they are lifetime transfers or transfers on death.

---

*"(1) A disposition is not a transfer of value if it is shown that it was not intended, and was not made in a transaction intended, to confer any gratuitous benefit on any person and either:

(a) that it was made in a transaction at arm's length between persons not connected with each other, or

(b) that it was such as might be expected to be made in a transaction at arm's length between persons not connected with each other..." (IHTA 1984 s10)

The spouse/civil partner exemption

As previously mentioned, transfers between spouses and civil partners are exempt from inheritance tax. Again, this applies to lifetime transfers and to transfers on death.

Note that for the exemption to apply, the parties must be legally married or have legally entered into a civil partnership. Merely cohabiting does not qualify for the exemption.

Gifts to charities

If you make a gift to a charity it will be exempt from inheritance tax*. In addition, if you make an outright gift to a trust that has been established for charitable purposes only, it will be exempt from inheritance tax. The gift will be exempt whether it is a lifetime gift or a gift in a will (i.e. a transfer on death).

The charity must be established in the UK. This means that it must be regulated by and subject to the laws and courts of the UK. In practice, this probably means that it is only safe to assume that an institution has charitable status for inheritance tax purposes if it is registered with the Charity Commission.

This is the position for any gift that most people would regard as 'straightforward'.

HMRC regard a gift as straightforward if "it is expressed as being given absolutely and unconditionally to a charity..."

Further, "[a] gift is considered not to be straightforward where:

- it is expressed to be for a special purpose, or
- it is for a subsidiary fund of an organisation..."**

The law being what it is, there are various rules to ensure that many gifts which are other than everyday and straightforward are not given the exemption. So to be certain that your gift will qualify for the exemption, it will be as well if you ensure that your gift is:

1. outright
2. immediate
3. to a UK-registered charity.

*IHTA 1984 s23
**HMRC IHT Manual – IHTM 11124

1. Outright

The gift must be outright. This means that it must not be subject to any conditions or limitations*.

*Although I have stated that the gift must be outright and subject to no restrictions or limitations, this point should perhaps be clarified. The safest course of action, if you want a gift to qualify for the charitable exemption, is to make an outright gift – i.e. an ordinary straightforward gift. However, the legislation does permit gifts that are less than outright to receive the benefit of the charitable exemption. There seems little possibility that many people would have cause to go down the route of making such a gift. However, for the few who may contemplate it, here is what the legislation has to say on the subject:

IHTA 1984 s23: "Gifts to charities

(1) Transfers of value are exempt to the extent that the values transferred by them are attributable to property which is given to charities.

(2) Subsection (1) above shall not apply in relation to property if the testamentary or other disposition by which it is given:

a. takes effect on the termination after the transfer of value of any interest or period, or
b. depends on a condition which is not satisfied within 12 months after the transfer, or
c. is defeasible;

and for this purpose any disposition which has not been defeated at a time twelve months after the transfer of value and is not defeasible after that time shall be treated as not being defeasible (whether or not it was capable of being defeated before that time).

(3) Subsection (1) above shall not apply in relation to property which is an interest in other property if:

a. that interest is less than the donor's, or
b. the property is given for a limited period;

and for this purpose any question whether an interest is less than the donor's shall be decided as at a time 12 months after the transfer of value.

(4) Subsection (1) above shall not apply in relation to any property if:

a. the property is land or a building and is given subject to an interest reserved or created by the donor which entitled him, his spouse [F1or civil partner] or a person connected with him to possession of, or to occupy, the whole or any part of the land or building rent-free or at a rent less than might be expected to be obtained in a transaction at arm's length between persons not connected with each other, or
b. the property is not land or a building and is given subject to an interest reserved or created by the donor other than:
   (i) an interest created by him for full consideration in money or money's worth, or
   (ii) an interest which does not substantially affect the enjoyment of the property by the person or body to whom it is given;

and for this purpose any question whether property is given subject to an interest shall be decided as at a time 12 months after the transfer of value.

(5) Subsection (1) above shall not apply in relation to property if it or any part of it may become applicable for purposes other than charitable purposes or those of a body mentioned in section 24, [F2 or 25] below [F3 or, where it is land, of a body mentioned in section 24A below].

(6) For the purposes of this section property is given to charities if it becomes the property of charities or is held on trust for charitable purposes only, and "donor" shall be construed accordingly."

2. Immediate

This means that there must be no prior interest in the gift – e.g. "I give my sister Jane a right to occupy my house until her death and after her death I give my house to ABC Registered Charity."

3. UK-registered charity

I.e. registered with the Charity Commission, and given a registered charity number.

Other gifts

Immediate outright gifts to the following are exempt whether lifetime transfers or on death:

- political parties (note that that this does not mean gifts to any political parties – the party must qualify*)
- housing associations**
- bodies established for national purposes***
- maintenance funds for historic buildings****.

---

*IHTA 1984 s24

**IHTA 1984 s24A

***IHTA 1984 s25

****IHTA 1984 s27

1.16.3 Transfers that are exempt only on death (active service)

There is a complete exemption from inheritance tax for estates of persons who die as a result of injuries or disease contracted while on active service in the armed forces*.

This exemption is perhaps more important and more widely available than may appear at first.

There was a widely reported case in 2007 in which the Manchester-based law firm Linder Myers saved a client more than £1m in inheritance tax by using the death in active service exemption. The exemption was claimed on the estate of an 83-year-old veteran of the Second World War. He sustained injuries in France in 1944 but did not die until 2005.

Although he died some 61 years after the injuries, the cause of death was shown to be linked to those injuries and a full exemption from IHT was granted.

There has been at least one case where the exemption has been used to reclaim tax that was needlessly paid on the estate of a veteran, so as to provide his widow's estate with a full transferable nil-rate band.

The *HMRC Inheritance Tax Manual* states that the conditions to be satisfied to claim the exemption are that the estate must be:

"...the death estate

- of a member of the armed forces or certain associated services
- whose death was caused by injury or disease received or aggravated while he or she was on active service.

*I.e. "the deceased was a member of any of the armed forces of the Crown or (not being a member of any of those forces) was subject to the law governing any of those forces by reason of association with or accompanying any body of those forces and (in any case) was either:

(a) on active service against an enemy, or

(b) on other service of a warlike nature or which in the opinion of the Treasury involved the same risks as service of a warlike nature." IHTA 1984 s154

The exemption applies only when the office receives a valid certificate...

Exemption must be given by the office on receipt of a valid certificate and cannot be given without it."

1.17 Reliefs available in respect of inheritance tax

Some forms of property are given reliefs from inheritance tax.

1.17.1 Business property relief (BPR)

Business property relief (usually referred to as 'BPR') is given to business property and can provide up to 100% relief from inheritance tax. In other words, the inheritance tax that would otherwise be payable on the value of business property and assets is reduced to nil. If you are a business owner, you cannot, however, assume that your business will attract the relief; there is a host of conditions to be met:

1. the business must be a qualifying business
2. the business property must be what is referred to as "relevant business property"; and
3. there is an ownership condition that has to be fulfilled.

1. Qualifying business

To be a qualifying business, the business must, broadly speaking, be a trading business rather than an investment business.

The business can include "a business carried on in the exercise of a profession *but does not include a business carried on otherwise than for gain*" [italics mine].

Most businesses carried on for profit will be likely to fall within the definition; however, there may be problems with what might be referred to as hobbyist or 'lifestyle businesses' (e.g. the sale of models of railway engines or military hardware) if there is little evidence of profit.

There are certain activities which are not qualifying businesses and it is important to be aware of these. They are: businesses that consist wholly or mainly of dealing in securities, stocks and shares, land or buildings or making or holding investments.

A buy-to-let business will be classed as an investment business and will not attract the relief.

If the business has mixed activities (e.g. a buy-to-let business which involves the provision of services to the tenants) then the "wholly or mainly" test might have to be considered:

> "A business or interest in a business, or shares in or securities of a company, are not relevant business property if the business or, as the case may be, the business carried out by the company consists wholly or mainly of one or more of the following, that is to say, dealing in securities, stocks or shares, land or buildings or making or holding investments."*

A buy-to-let business would clearly fail the "wholly or mainly" test. But if the provision of services for tenants was arranged via a separate company and paid for separately, the separate company might attract business property relief.

Some businesses appear to be borderline and may in some cases attract the relief and in others not. Caravan parks are probably the main case in point, and attract the relief, or fail to attract it, based on whether the income is derived mainly from rent or mainly from the provision of other services.

*IHTA 105 (3)

2. Relevant business property

Some forms of business property – referred to as "relevant business property" – are given the relief at 100% and others at 50%.

Relevant business property which is given the relief at 100%:

- a business (e.g. a sole proprietor*) or an interest in a business (e.g. a partnership interest)
- unquoted shares in a company (at one time unquoted shares would only receive the benefit of 50% BPR unless they conferred control of the company immediately before the transfer)
- unquoted securities in a company which gave the transferor control of the company immediately before the transfer (he might have given some away prior to the transfer in question – the point is that he must now be giving away sufficient securities to confer control).

Relevant business property which is given the relief at 50%:

- quoted shares which gave the transferor control of the company
- land, buildings, machinery or plant used by a company controlled by the transferor or by a partnership of which the transferor was a member
- land, buildings, machinery or plant held in a trust in which the transferor had an interest in possession and which was used in his business (this applies to lifetime transfers of such things *only* and will probably diminish in importance with the passage of time due to the effects of the Finance Act 2006).

---

*A sole proprietor is an individual who owns his business outright with no partners and with no limited company.

3. Ownership condition

The relevant business property must have been owned for a minimum of two years immediately prior to the date of the transfer. This provision could deter some business owners from investing in their own businesses and perhaps for this reason the ownership condition is extended to cover relevant business property which has replaced, directly or indirectly, other relevant business property. (If the periods of ownership together of the original and replacement relevant business property comprise a total of two years within the five years immediately prior to the transfer.)

1.17.2 Clawback – a dangerous pitfall for a recipient of a business

If you have a business which qualifies for BPR and you do not require either the income of the business or the proceeds of the sale of the business, there is a case to be made for giving it away to the next generation some time before passing away.

If you give away your business while it qualifies for the protective cover of BPR, you will be able to make the gift free of inheritance tax. (But do not simply take that statement at face value – read this entire section then revisit it!)

The case to be made is that BPR may not be available in the future*, and you might as well take advantage of it while you know that it can be used to your advantage to get the value of your business out of your taxable estate.

However, this case comes with an important rider.

The BPR that was allowed on the gift can be lost after the date of the gift depending on subsequent events.

*Two reasons that BPR may not be available in the future are (1) that your business may evolve into a different kind of business in which trading activities may not be predominant; and (2) a future government may move the goalposts in such a way that your business no longer qualifies for BPR even if the nature of the business does not change significantly. Or at all.

If you die within seven years of giving away your business, BPR will be lost if the recipient of your gift has disposed of the business property without replacing it, other than if the disposal were the result of his own death.

If the recipient has disposed of the business property in the circumstances described above, *inheritance tax will be payable on the original gift as if BPR had not applied to it.*

This is known as clawback. It is one of the ways in which BPR differs from an exemption. An exempt transfer will not be affected by subsequent events.

1.17.3 Giving away a business you have sold or are selling

If you have read about the clawback provisions (1.17.2 above) you might think that a handy way around them could be to sell the business, then give away the proceeds of sale; or to give away your business subject to a binding contract for sale, so that the recipient receives the sale proceeds. This could theoretically (you might think) have the advantage that the disposal of the business would not be an event subsequent to the gifting of it (since you have either sold it first, or united the two stages in one), and so would not be affected by the clawback provisions.

While this line of reasoning is essentially correct, HMRC has no need for the clawback provisions in these situations as BPR firstly does not apply to the proceeds of sale of a business, and secondly does not apply to a business which is given away whilst subject to a binding contract for sale.

Note that, although in this, and the preceding section, I have referred to giving away the business, and to the recipient, these comments apply to all forms of lifetime transfers of a business to all forms of transferee, e.g. sale at an undervalue to the transferee.

1.17.4 Agricultural property relief (APR)

APR is given automatically for transfers of agricultural property. Unlike BPR, it does not apply to all classes of asset, only to land and buildings.

Agricultural property is defined as "agricultural land or pasture and includes woodland and any building used in connection with the intensive rearing of livestock or fish if the woodland or building is occupied with agricultural land or pasture and the occupation is ancillary to that of the agricultural land or pasture; and also includes such cottages, farm buildings and farmhouses, together with the land occupied with them, as are of a character appropriate to the property."*

The relief is only given in respect of the agricultural value of the property (as opposed to the open market value, which may be higher).

It applies to property which was either:

- occupied by the transferor for agricultural purposes throughout the two years immediately prior to the transfer; or
- owned by the transferor for the seven years immediately prior to the transfer and occupied by someone (whether the transferor or someone else) for agricultural purposes throughout the seven year period.

Farmhouses must be of an appropriate character to be granted the relief – a point of much contention. HMRC are quick to distinguish farmhouses that lack (in their view) "appropriate character".

Details of how HMRC apply the "appropriate character" test are to be found in on the HMRC website in the *Inheritance Tax Manual*, (**www.hmrc.gov.uk/manuals/ihtmanual/IHTM24051.htm**) which states at IHTM 24051:

*IHTA 1984 s115

"The main factors to be applied when determining whether a farmhouse is of a 'character appropriate' are considered to be:

- Is the farmhouse appropriate when judged by ordinary ideas of what is appropriate in size, layout, content, style and quality of construction in relation to the associated land and buildings?
- Is the farmhouse proportionate in size and nature to the requirements of the agricultural activities conducted on the agricultural land? You should bear in mind that different types of agricultural operation require different amounts of land. This is an aspect on which the VOA [Valuation Office Agency] will be able to give advice.
- Within the agricultural land, does the land predominate so that the farmhouse is ancillary to the land?
- Would a reasonable and informed person regard the property simply as a house with land or as a farmhouse?
- Applying the "elephant test", would you recognise this as a farmhouse if you saw it? Although this test involves some subjectivity, it can be useful in ruling out extremes at either end of the scale.
- How long has the farmhouse and agricultural property been associated and is there a history of agricultural production? The matter has to be decided on the facts that existed as at the date of death or transfer but evidence of the farmhouse having previously been occupied with a larger area of land may be relevant evidence.
- Considering the relationship between the value of the house and the profitability of the land, would the house attract demand from a commercial farmer who has to earn a living from the land, or is its value significantly out of proportion to the profitability of the land? If business accounts have been supplied, copies should be forwarded to the VOA. Business

accounts can give a useful indication of the extent of the agricultural activity being carried on (although a loss-making enterprise is not on its own considered to be a determinative factor).

- Considering all other relevant factors, including whether any land is let out and on what terms, is the scale of the agricultural operations in context?
- There must be some connection or nexus between "such cottages, farm buildings and farmhouses, together with the land occupied with them" and the property to which they must be of a character appropriate. The argument that the nexus must be derived from common ownership rather than common occupation was accepted by the Special Commissioner in Rosser v Inland Revenue Commissioners [2003] STC (SCD) 311."

100% relief is given if the transferor had right to vacant possession immediately before the transfer, or the right to obtain it within the 12 months following the transfer; or (by concession) if the transferor had right to vacant possession within 24 months of the transfer. 100% is also given if the property is let on a tenancy commencing on or after 1 September 1995 (in other words, if the property is rented out by the owner to someone else).

50% relief is given in all other cases.

Prior to 22 April 2009, APR could only be claimed for agricultural property in the UK, the Channel Islands and the Isle of Man. The Finance Act 2009 extended the application of the relief. For transfers of value on or after 22 April 2009, APR can now be claimed in respect of agricultural property in the UK, the Channel Islands, the Isle of Man, and land in states within the European Economic Area (EEA) but outside the UK.

Moreover, APR can be claimed retrospectively for any inheritance tax due or paid on or after 23 April 2003 on qualifying agricultural property within the EEA. The claim must be made on or before:

- the date determined under section 241(1) of the IHTA84* as the last date on which the claim may be made, or
- 21 April 2010 (whichever is later).

1.17.5 Woodlands relief

Woodlands relief does not reduce the IHT payable on woodlands; it allows the payment of IHT to be deferred, potentially for long periods of time, and it applies to the value of the timber rather than the land.

There are ownership conditions to be satisfied.

Woodlands relief is available only on death and must be applied for by the Personal Representatives (PRs) of the deceased within two years of the date of death.

1.18 Capital gains tax (CGT)

Although this is a book about inheritance tax, some discussion of the capital gains tax (CGT) regime is essential to help you to avoid certain unpleasant consequences with regard to PETs. Namely, the inadvertent triggering of a charge to CGT when you make a PET.

---

*s241 states: "— (1) If it is proved to the satisfaction of the Board that too much tax has been paid on the value transferred by a chargeable transfer or on so much of that value as is attributable to any property, the Board shall repay the excess unless the claim for repayment was made more than six years after the date on which the payment or last payment of the tax was made.

(2) References in this section to tax include references to interest on tax."

CGT is not charged on gifts of cash. Therefore a PET in the form of cash or a cheque will not trigger adverse CGT consequences.

CGT is not charged on your home (or, if you have more than one home, the home that you occupy as your main residence). This is called main residence relief; it is why you can sell your home without having to pay CGT.

CGT, as the name suggests, is a tax on the gain in value of an asset. The charge does not arise until the asset is disposed of.

Example

Joe buys shares in a company which has always been a favourite with all manner of financial advisors, called Fairytale Growth Plc. He pays £50,000 for the shares. Five years later he still owns the shares, which (somewhat to the surprise of his financial advisor, who strangely did not invest in the company himself) are now worth £500,000. He will not pay CGT, even though his shares have risen in value tenfold. This is because he has not disposed of the shares. There will only be a charge to CGT if or when he disposes of them.

Joe decides to sell the shares. This, as most people are aware, will trigger a charge to CGT.

What is less widely appreciated is that if Joe decides against selling the shares, and instead gives them to his daughter Amanda, this will also trigger a charge to CGT. *A gift is just as much a disposal of property for CGT purposes as a sale.*

How much CGT will Joe pay on the shares?

When you acquire an asset, whether you buy it or receive it as a gift, it has a value on the date that you acquire it. This is known as the base value. CGT is charged on the difference between the base value and the value of the asset at the date you dispose of it, known as the gain.

CGT is not charged on the entire difference between the two values.

In the tax year 2009-2010, individuals had an annual allowance of £10,100. This meant that anyone who disposed of an asset would not have to pay CGT on the gain if the gain was £10,100 or less.

In the tax year 2010, there was a flat rate for CGT of 18%.*

If Joe had disposed of his shares in the tax year 2009-10, the first £10,100 of the gain in value from £50,000 to £500,000 would have been CGT-free due to his annual allowance (if he had not made any other disposals that year) and the (significant!) remainder would have been taxed at 18%.

It is likely that, whatever else happens with CGT, there will always be an annual exemption, and that main residence relief will always continue to apply. I.e. if you own only one house and you live in it as your permanent residence and you sell it, there will be no CGT to pay**.

In the immediate future, it is likely that the coalition government will increase the rate of CGT to 40% to bring it in line with income tax (the declared aim of the government). And it is likely that there will be an array of complicated measures providing relief for some business assets.

CGT is not charged on death. Death is arguably a good thing where CGT is concerned!

*Until 23 June 2010 when the emergency budget put in place by the coalition government introduced a 28% rate in addition to the 18% rate, Joe is assumed to pay the 18% rate!

**The main residence relief does not apply in all cases to all homes. It may not apply to the whole property if you own more than 0.5 hectares; if you have extensive outbuildings; if you have used part of it exclusively for business purposes; or if you have bought the home purely for the purpose of selling it at a profit.

Example

If Joe does not sell or give away his shares in Fairytale Growth Plc, but dies while owning them and leaves them in his will to his daughter, their increased value of £500,000 will be a transfer for inheritance tax purposes. However, it (the transfer on death) will not be a disposal for CGT purposes, even though Joe is effectively giving up his ownership of the shares. Joe's daughter will acquire the shares without having to pay CGT on them.

If Joe was a widower and his executors had his nil-rate band and the transferable nil-rate band of his late wife, Amanda might receive the shares without paying any inheritance tax on them.

What is the base value of the shares when Amanda receives them? It is the value they had at the date of Joe's death. If the shares do not rise in value in the months following Joe's death and Amanda sells them fairly promptly, there will be no CGT to pay on them. If the shares continue their meteoric rise in value and Amanda sells them, CGT will be charged on the gain that has occurred since Joe's death.

It may be noted somewhat heartlessly that Joe's death could be said to have had favourable CGT consequences. The base value when Amanda disposed of the shares was not the £50,000 that Joe paid, but the higher value of £500,000 that they had on his death. The CGT that she might pay on any subsequent further rise in value was correspondingly less than Joe would have paid had he lived to sell the shares.

Planning issue

If you are making any gift other than a gift of cash or cheque, always consider the CGT consequences and take advice from your accountant if appropriate.

Note that in Part 2, a means is indicated of gifting assets that are ripe with gain without suffering the CGT consequences.

1.19 Associated operations

It might be possible to avoid inheritance tax by making one or more transactions (usually of an artificial nature) to reduce the value of an asset, then transferring that asset to another person.

There are anti-avoidance provisions to prevent this. These provisions are generally known as 'associated operations'.

Associated operations have the effect that all the transactions made in a series will be treated as one single transaction, made at the time of the last transaction; and that the donor will be deemed to have reduced his estate in value by the amount that it has been reduced by *all* the transactions which have reduced it in total.

1.20 Gifts with a reservation of benefit

As has been explained, inheritance tax can be avoided by making gifts of money, property and assets to other people.

It may occur to some readers of this book who do not want to give away their wealth but who nevertheless want to avoid inheritance tax that they might arrange their affairs in such a way as to cease to be owners of some of their wealth but nevertheless continue to enjoy it.

The classic example is the transfer of the family home to the children, while continuing to live in it.

Sadly, this approach will not bring about the desired reduction in inheritance tax.

Generally, if an individual gives away his home to his child or children and continues to occupy it, then on his death his family home will be subject to inheritance tax. The amount of tax payable may not be the same as it would have been had he retained ownership of it. It may be higher.

This is because the possibility that some people might arrange their affairs in this way has been legislated for. The regime that has been put in place to prevent this labels this type of transaction as a "gift with a reservation of benefit", or a GROB. It applies to all forms of property, not merely to houses.

A GROB occurs when:

> "an individual disposes of any property by way of gift and either:
>
> (a) possession and enjoyment of the property is not bona fide assumed by the donee [i.e. the receiver of the gift] at or before the beginning of the relevant period; or
>
> (b) at any time in the relevant period the property is not enjoyed to the entire exclusion, or virtually to the entire exclusion, of the donor and of any benefit to him by contract or otherwise;
>
> and in this section 'the relevant period' means a period ending on the date of the donor's death and beginning seven years before that date or, if it is later, on the date of the gift."
>
> (Finance Act 1986)

The GROB rules will catch many transactions of the 'have your cake and eat it' variety.

The result of the GROB rules can actually be to make matters worse than if the GROB had never been made. This can be especially true with a GROB of the family home, where not only will there be no improvement in the IHT position (and possibly a worsening of it) there will also be the loss of the main residence exemption for CGT purposes.

The reason that the GROB provisions can worsen the IHT situation is that on death, if the gifted asset is still subject to a reservation, the inheritance tax treatment can be harsh. The tax due on the GROB is arrived at by making two calculations, one on the basis that the asset had never been gifted, and is taxed as part of the death estate; the second on the basis that that the transfer actually did take place. The calculation of the two that produces the biggest charge to inheritance tax is used to determine the tax due on the gifted asset.

There have been a number of attempts to circumvent the GROB rules over the years, some of them successful, with the result that HMRC has introduced other measures (e.g. pre-owned assets tax – see 1.19) to prevent transactions which attempt to get around the GROB rules.

Exemptions to the GROB rules

There is a small range of situations in which the GROB rules do not apply, notwithstanding that on the face of it a gift may involve a reservation of benefit.

Exemption where there is full consideration

Where an individual gives away land or an interest in land and continues to occupy the land or to enjoy the interest in the land, his occupation or enjoyment will be disregarded if he pays for it.

He must pay the full market value that the occupation of the land or enjoyment of the interest in the land would fetch on the open market. (In other words, he must pay a market value rent or the equivalent consideration in money's worth).

Similarly, if the individual has given away a chattel and is in possession of the chattel, his possession will be disregarded for IHT purposes if he pays in full the market value for his possession of it.

This exemption can open up planning opportunities for the small number of individuals who are sufficiently wealthy to give away amenities and then to rent the amenities they once owned. (And who are not averse to doing so.)

Exemption where there is a change of circumstances

If an individual has given away land and ceased to occupy it, he may be able to resume occupation without triggering the GROB rules, if his occupation is due to a change in circumstances. This exemption applies to situations such as that where a father gives a house to his son or to another relative and moves elsewhere, but is then obliged to return and live in the house (with the agreement of the donee) due to a change of circumstances that was unforeseen at the time the gift was made.

"In the case of property which is an interest in land, any occupation by the donor of the whole, or any part of the land, shall be disregarded if:

(i) it results from a change in circumstances of the donor since the time of the gift, being a change which was unforeseen at the time and was not brought about by the donor to receive the benefit of this provision; and

(ii) it occurs at a time when the donor has become unable to maintain himself through old age, infirmity or otherwise; and

(iii) it represents a reasonable provision by the donee for the care and maintenance of the donor; and

(iv) the donee is a relative of the donor or his spouse."*

Note that the donee may be a relative – apparently any relative – of the donor or his spouse or civil partner and that the change in circumstances must involve the donor being unable to maintain himself. The inability can be due to old age, infirmity "or otherwise" which appears to be wide ranging.

Whether wide ranging enough to include being hard up probably remains to be seen.

These rules cannot be interpreted, for instance, to mean that parents may give their house to their children and keep living there in retirement without penalty. They would have to move out first, then move back in, due to being unable to maintain themselves as a result of old age or infirmity or some other good reason.

---

*Finance Act 1986 Schedule 20 6(1)(b)

Other miscellaneous exemptions

The GROB rules do not apply if the transfer is exempt as:

- a small gift
- a gift in consideration of marriage
- a charitable gift
- a gift to a housing association
- a gift to maintenance funds for historic buildings
- a gift for national purposes
- a gift to a political party
- a gift to an employee benefit trust
- a gift to a spouse or civil partner which is exempt because of the spouse exemption (in very unusual and highly technical circumstances it may be possible for the GROB rules to apply to gifts involving spouses and civil partners. But it is probable that you can safely ignore this possibility)*.

Planning issue

Bear in mind the GROB rules when making gifts and take advice if you are considering making a gift which may possibly fall foul of those rules.

*Please excuse the following, which will read like gobbledegook unless you first read section 1.24 which is about trusts. The GROB rules would probably only apply to a gift exempt by way of the spouse exemption if the subject matter of the gift were to be placed in trust. It would have to be a lifetime trust which was not a relevant property trust, and the spouse exemption would have to apply because the spouse or civil partner had an interest in possession. This would be a highly implausible state of affairs, because it seems it is now impossible to create a lifetime trust with an interest in possession which is not a relevant property trust. But it is just possible that someone, somewhere will think of a way of doing it.

1.21 Pre-owned assets

You might think that, with the rules on associated operations and gifts with a reservation of benefit, it would be impossible, in fact, to cook up a scheme that allows an individual to artificially avoid inheritance tax. (E.g. by purporting to gift it but continuing in reality to make use of it.)

It is close to being impossible nowadays, but not for lack of trying on the part of solicitors in the past. Such is the ingenuity of tax planning lawyers that, over the years, they devised a number of complex schemes to get round the rules on associated operations and reservation of benefit. Such schemes allowed the users of them to live in their family homes after giving away the value in those homes, and to enjoy nevertheless the benefits of a significant reduction in inheritance tax.

Enter the pre-owned asset charge.

The pre-owned asset charge is a charge which appears to be intended to end once and for all the practice by well-advised individuals of gifting property to reduce their liability to inheritance tax, while continuing to enjoy benefits amounting almost to ownership of the property that has been gifted.

Although the pre-owned assets charge is applied in the context of schemes which are intended to reduce inheritance tax, it is not a charge to inheritance tax but a form of income tax.

Broadly speaking, the tax is applied to property that an individual enjoys which was once part of his estate, but is no longer part of his estate for inheritance tax purposes. There are three different charging regimes, one for land, one for chattels and one for intangibles.

The level of the charge represents, or is intended to represent, the value of the benefit in the property enjoyed by the taxpayer. Hence the charge on land is based on the rental value of the land.

The tax is retroactive, in that it applies to schemes that were created and set up prior to the legislation.

A full review of the pre-owned assets scheme is beyond the scope of this book. The above overview is a bare outline to bring to your attention the pitfalls of trying to artificially avoid inheritance tax.

1.22 Wills

At one time wills played a vital role in inheritance tax planning for many people. The importance of wills has been reduced since the introduction of the transferable nil-rate band, but they nevertheless continue to have an important role to play. Even if IHT were not an issue, a will would be a critical document for most people to make. Some kind of basic understanding of wills is therefore essential for anyone considering tax planning.

This section is not intended to give you anything resembling a comprehensive understanding of wills, merely to equip you with the minimum amount of knowledge that you will require in order to get to grips with the concept of wills.

The basic issues that you will need to be aware of are as follows:

1.22.1 A will only takes effect on death

Many people struggle initially to grasp this idea. They seem to think that a will, once signed, is a binding legal document. It may be, if the person who signed it dies. Until then, it has no legal impact*. It does not in any way determine the destination of the property of the person who signed it until that person dies.

The person who signed the will (known as a 'testator' if male and a 'testatrix' if female) is free to give away any item of property mentioned in the will and free to make a new will cancelling the will made already made at any time prior to death.

---

*The one exception to this rule is where two individuals make mutual wills and one of them dies without either of them having revoked (cancelled) their wills. In this situation, the will of the survivor becomes binding even though he or she is still alive. However, this position is rarely encountered.

1.22.2 A will takes effect over all the property owned at death

If properly written, a will should dispose of all the money, property and assets you own at the date of death. The acquisition of an asset during your lifetime should not generally necessitate re-writing your will on the grounds that the asset is not mentioned in your will. It may, however, necessitate re-writing your will if you intend the item of property to be given to a particular person who would not receive it under the terms of your current will.

1.22.3 A will can be used to make many different types of gift

You can use your will to give away specific items of property, e.g.:

> *"I give my Rolex watch to Sam."**

You can give specific sums of money, e.g.:

> *"I give £10,000 to Anthony."**

You can gift sums of money calculated by reference to a formula, e.g.:

> *"I give the largest sum of cash that can be taken from my estate without incurring a charge to IHT."*; or*
>
> *"I give a sum of money equal to the transferable nil-rate band of my late husband Charlie that is available to be claimed by my executors."**

You can make gifts by reference to the reliefs available to them, e.g.:

> *"I give all my business property which qualifies for 100% business property relief to Xavier."**

You can make gifts to individuals, to charities and political parties etc, and you can set up trusts (see 1.24) by means of your will.

1.22.4 Residue

The 'residue' or 'residuary estate' is everything that is left over after the payment of debts, funeral expenses, legal and administration expenses and specific gifts and gifts of money (such as those gifts in 1.22.3). A professionally drawn-up will always includes a clause giving away the residue, e.g.:

> *"I give my residuary estate to my wife Sarah."**

1.22.5 A will can be used to appoint executors and trustees

When you make your will, you need to give some consideration as to who will physically make sure that your wishes are carried out. E.g. if you have left your Rolex watch to Sam, someone will have to retrieve it from amongst your belongings and give it to Sam. Similarly, if you have created a trust in your will, someone has to be named to administer the trust.

The individuals who carry out the wishes expressed in your will are called executors; the individuals who administer trusts created in your will are called trustees.

The distinction can be important but is difficult to explain, and a complete explanation is beyond the scope of this book. Suffice it to say for now that in practice in the majority of cases the same individuals will be named to act both as executors and as trustees, e.g:

> *"I appoint my brother Ted and my nephew Alex as executors and trustees of this my will."**

1.22.6 A will can be used to appoint guardians of minor children

This is really not a tax planning issue at all but well worth knowing if you are making a will. If you are a parent and you have minor children, you will probably wish to provide for their welfare in the broadest sense, not simply their financial welfare. You can use a will to appoint people to look after your children – i.e. guardians.

> *"I appoint Mike Todd and his wife Sarah to be guardians of my infant child or children."**

*These are examples only of will clauses and not suggested wordings; you should not use the examples as the basis for drafting wills, but instead refer to an advisor or (if you really must draft your will yourself, which is not advisable) refer to a specialist text.

1.22.7 Common misconception

It is a common misconception that couples who are married or in a civil partnership make a single document which suffices as a will for both of them.

If they are drawn up by a professional, wills for couples who are married or in a civil partnership (or for that matter who are unmarried and living as partners) will always take the form of two separate documents, one for each spouse (or civil partnership or partner).

There have been instances of home-made wills made by married couples which have consisted of one document signed by both of them, but this is a rarity and does not set a precedent which should be followed.

1.23 Severance of tenancy

Severance of tenancy* is a concept that goes hand in hand with wills.

When two or more people are beneficial owners of a property, they can legally own the property** in two different ways. They can hold it as joint tenants or as tenants in common.

Joint tenants

If two people own a house as joint tenants and one of them dies, the surviving joint owner will automatically own the share of the house previously owned by the deceased joint owner.

Even if the deceased joint owner has left a will stating that his share of the house will be given to someone other than to the surviving joint owner, the surviving joint owner will *still* inherit the entire house. This is due to an action of law known as 'rights of survivorship'.

*The expressions "tenancy" and "tenants" in this context have nothing to do with renting a house or a flat or paying rent of any kind for any property whatsoever

**Property is being used in its widest sense and can refer to a house, bank account, shareholding or virtually any other asset

Tenants in common

If two people own a house as tenants in common and one of them dies, the surviving joint owner will *not* automatically inherit the share of the house owned by the deceased joint owner. The person who inherits the share of the house will be determined by the will of the deceased owner (if he has made one) or the rules which apply when there is no will (known as the rules of intestacy).

Changing a joint tenancy to a tenancy in common (severance of tenancy)

It is possible to change a joint tenancy to a tenancy in common in a number of ways. The most important of these ways and the one most used in practice is for one of the joint owners to serve a notice (known as a 'notice of severance') on the other joint owner.

This is known as 'severance of tenancy'.

If the property in question is a house or a flat which is registered with the land registry, the land registry must be notified using a document known as an SEV 1.

Conclusion

It follows that if you are a joint owner of anything and you are happy for the surviving joint owner to inherit that thing, you may safely own it as a joint tenant. If, however, you want to be able to use your will to direct your share of the jointly owned property to someone else, you will have to own the property as a tenant in common. This may involve severing the tenancy.

The ability to direct in your will who would inherit your share of a jointly owned property, especially a share in the family home, was of prime importance (at least for tax-planning purposes) prior to the introduction of the transferable nil-rate band. It may still have some application today, e.g. where the owners of (say) a house are neither married nor in a civil partnership. This will be explored later (at 2.12).

Although this section has focused on one aspect of joint ownership, namely some of the inheritance issues surrounding jointly held property, it should be noted that there is rather more to joint ownership than the material in this section. This section is intended to give the general reader no more than the minimum required to consider how joint ownership might affect inheritance, and hence tax planning by means of a will.

One point worth adding is that severance of tenancy is probably an issue that gives rise to more negligence claims against solicitors than almost anything else. It is all too easy to draft a will which gives away a share of a jointly owned house, then fail to sever the tenancy, or at least to correctly sever it, with the result that the surviving joint owner inherits the share of the house of the deceased joint owner, and the beneficiary who should have received it is disappointed. And sues.

1.24 Trusts

It is important to have a basic understanding of trusts if you are contemplating using a trust in conjunction with inheritance tax planning.

1.24.1 Definition of a trust

There is no simple all-embracing definition of a trust in English law. Moreover, there are several different types of trust that arise in different circumstances.

1.24.2 Explanation of the concept of a trust

These are examples of a lifetime trusts which may help you to get to grips with the concept.

Example

If I were very wealthy and generous, I might decide that I wanted to provide some form of financial benefit for certain relatives of mine – for instance, an elderly aunt and two young nephews.

I might decide on the provision of a fund of £1,000,000 to assist them.

But I might not want to give them the money directly, without putting in place some form of restriction on how it might be used.

I might have many motives for wishing to place restrictions on the availability of the money, and the uses to which it might be put.

In the case of my aunt, I might be worried about the prospect of her going into long-term care, in which case the money I had given her would be (from my point of view) wasted on paying care home fees.

In the case of my nephews, I might be concerned that if they married young and were subsequently divorced, a young woman that I did not care for might get her hands on a substantial sum of my money in the form of a divorce settlement.

Rather than take these risks, I could put the money in a trust for the benefit of my aunt and nephews.

I would probably go about it by seeing a solicitor and having him prepare a document stating that I wanted a sum of money (known as a trust fund) to be used for the benefit of my aunt and nephews.

The document could name two people to look after the trust fund – perhaps you and a friend of yours.

Then I could give you and your friend the £1,000,000 and ask you both to read the document that I had prepared and to use the money in the way that the document stipulated to help my aunt and nephews.

On reading the document you might discover that you were to consider the needs of my aunt and nephews from time to time, then use your discretion to give each of them such sums of money from time to time as seemed appropriate to their needs.

The trust document might empower you to give or lend money to my aunt and nephews, to grant them an income from the trust fund or give them lump sums of capital, and to purchase houses on their behalf.

You will note from this that a trust has three ingredients:

1. trustees (yourself and your friend in the example)
2. a trust fund (my £1,000,000); and
3. beneficiaries (my aunt and nephews).

It also (usually) has a document, known as a trust deed, which sets out how the trust is to be run.

In my example, you and your friend, being the trustees, would be responsible for looking after the trust fund and for running the trust. Although you would legally own the £1,000,000 that I had given to you, you would not be permitted to spend the money on yourselves, only on my aunt and nephews.

As I had not told you what share of the trust fund each of the beneficiaries was to be given, and had left it to your discretion to decide how much money to give to each beneficiary and when, I would have created a form of trust known as a 'discretionary trust'.

* * *

If, in the above example, I had told you to pay the interest generated by the trust fund to my aunt for her life, and to pay the capital to my nephews on her death, it would have been a 'life interest trust'. (Known also as a 'fixed interest trust' or an 'interest in possession trust').

My aunt would have been known as the 'life tenant' and my nephews would have had 'an interest in remainder' or a 'remainder interest'.

(We will see that, somewhat confusingly, the above trusts could also be called 'relevant property trusts'.)

A trust can be set up by a person during his or her lifetime, as in my example, in which case it is known as a (lifetime trust) or (settlement) and the document creating it is known as a (trust deed) or (declaration of trust).

A trust can also be created in a will, in which case it is known as a (will trust). There is usually no separate trust or settlement deed with a will trust, as the will itself sets out the terms of the trust. However, sometimes a person creates a lifetime trust then directs in his will that on his death money should be paid into the trust from his estate.

1.24.3 Types of trust

Discretionary trust

As explained in 1.24.2.

A discretionary trust can be created as a lifetime trust or as a will trust.

Life interest trust

As explained in 1.24.2.

A life interest trust can be created as a lifetime trust or as a will trust.

Transitional serial interest

This is a life interest trust created prior to 22 March 2006, in which the life interest has been redirected from the life tenant to another life tenant. As this book is not a specialist text on trusts, no more will be said on the matter.

Flexible life interest trust (FLIT)

This is a trust in which one person (known as the 'life tenant') is entitled to the income from the trust fund, and one or more people are entitled to the capital of the trust fund on the death of the life tenant.

What distinguishes this from a life interest trust is that the trustees have wide ranging powers to terminate the interest of the life tenant and to give the entitlement to life interest to another beneficiary, and to distribute capital to beneficiaries.

A FLIT can be created as a lifetime trust or as a will trust.

Life Interest further explained

Although I have referred to a life interest as an entitlement to the income of a trust fund, this has been done purely for the purposes of assisting with an explanation of the concept. A life interest has a wider application than an entitlement to income and arises in other situations besides those when an individual has a right to the income of a trust fund.

The right to the income (or other benefit) is referred to as an 'interest in possession'.

An interest in possession does not consist of outright ownership of money, property or assets. It is an immediate and continuing right to derive some benefit from them in some way.

A life interest has been defined as a "present right to present enjoyment" and can include (for instance) the right to occupy a house.

Immediate post-death interest trust (IPDI trust)

An IPDI trust is a trust that can only be created when a death occurs. It may be created by a will, or, if there is no will, it may be created by the rules which apply in the absence of a will, known as intestacy rules. It cannot be created by a person during his or her lifetime. It can only be created on death.

It is a trust in which a beneficiary is entitled to something less than an absolute gift of money or an asset; usually the beneficiary will have a right to the income or interest from an asset, rather than an asset itself. This right is known as an interest in possession.

An IPDI trust currently receives potentially favourable tax treatment as compared with a trust on the same terms created by a person while he is still alive. (Technically referred to as a 'living settlor'.) There are a number of qualifying factors to be observed for a trust to be treated as an IPDI trust.

The *Inheritance Tax Manual* is a good source of free information on this and other trust matters. Go to **www.hmrc.gov.uk**, and find the section on manuals. The *Inheritance Tax Manual* is the one you need. Refer to sections IHTM16060 onwards. IPDI trusts are specifically mentioned at IHTM16061.

Trusts for bereaved minors/18-25 trusts

Trusts for bereaved minors/18-25 trusts are trusts that can only be created by a will or intestacy. They must be created by the will or intestacy of a deceased parent or under the criminal injuries compensation scheme. They can only be created on death.

The beneficiaries must become entitled to the trust property on attaining 25 or earlier.

Disabled trust

A disabled trust is a trust for the benefit of a person who is incapable of managing his own affairs.

There are many qualifying factors to be observed for a trust to be treated as a disabled trust.

A disabled trust can be created as a lifetime trust or as a will trust.

Protective trust

A protective trust is a trust set up to give a life interest to a beneficiary, in which (to prevent trust money being squandered by the beneficiary) the life interest is forfeited if the beneficiary becomes bankrupt or attempts to dispose of it in some specifically prohibited way.

A protective trust can be created as a lifetime trust or as a will trust.

Settlor-interested trusts

A settlor* is a person who sets up a trust and puts money, property or assets into the trust.

A settlor-interested trust is a trust in which the person who created the trust, or his wife or civil partner or minor children**, can take a benefit. This situation is seldom desirable. Settlor-interested trusts may be subject to worse IHT and CGT treatment than any other kind of trust. Section 2.6 will inform you of a method of mitigating the impact of CGT by using trusts to qualify for a tax relief known as holdover relief. If a trust has qualified for, and been given the benefit of, holdover relief for CGT at some time in the past, and subsequently becomes settlor-interested, the results can be financially catastrophic. The holdover relief may be clawed back by HMRC.

A settlor-interested trust is by definition a creature created during the lifetime of the settlor. If he were dead, he could not have an interest in the trust.

---

*The word 'settlor' is given a very wide meaning for IHT purposes:

"(1) In this Act "settlor", in relation to a settlement, includes any person by whom the settlement was made directly or indirectly, and in particular (but without prejudice to the generality of the preceding words) includes any person who has provided funds directly or indirectly for the purpose of or in connection with the settlement or has made with any other person a reciprocal arrangement for that other person to make the settlement.

"(2) Where more than one person is a settlor in relation to a settlement and the circumstances so require, this Part of this Act (except section 48(4) to (6)) shall have effect in relation to it as if the settled property were comprised in separate settlements." (IHTA 1984 s44)

**Legislation that came into effect on 6 April 2006 has caused trusts to be settlor-interested trusts if the beneficiaries of those trusts included the settlor's minor children.

Bare trust

This is a trust in which one person quite simply holds property on behalf of another person. E.g. if I gave you £500 cash and asked you to hold it on behalf of my son and give it to him if he requested it, you would hold the £500 as a bare trustee. You would have no powers over the money and would be obliged to give it to my son at his request.

A bare trust can be created as a lifetime trust or as a will trust.

IHT and trusts

The inheritance tax charges on trusts are far from straightforward. The following sections give an outline of the tax treatment.

IHT treatment of all trusts created prior to 22 March 1986

Prior to March 1986 there were three IHT regimes for trusts. If a trust had an interest in possession, it was subject to the interest in possession regime (1); if it had no interest in possession, it was subject to the relevant property regime (2). The third regime was a favourable regime for trusts created for children and young people, known as accumulation and maintenance trusts. Accumulation and maintenance trusts can no longer be created and have more or less been phased out.

1. Interest in possession trust IHT regime

Prior to 22 March 2006, a beneficiary with an interest in possession was treated for IHT purposes as the beneficial owner of the trust fund.

Hence:

1. a transfer into the trust was a PET
2. when the life tenant died the trust fund would be aggregated with his estate and the total value would be subject to IHT

3. a termination of the life interest during the lifetime of the life tenant would be a PET.

If an interest in possession trust was created prior to 22 March 2006, it will remain subject to the above regime.

2. Relevant property trust IHT regime

The main features of the relevant property regime are as follows:

- Any transfer into such a trust is a chargeable transfer at the time of the transfer.
- As noted in 1.15.4, where a lifetime chargeable transfer was made after 5 April and prior to 1 October in any year, the 20% tax (if any) is due on 30 April in the following year; where the transfer was made after 30 September and prior to 6 April in any year, the 20% tax (if any) is due six months after the end of the month in which the transfer was made.
- There are exit charges on property leaving such trusts. Property leaves the trusts on those occasions that the trustees decide to give money, property and assets to the beneficiaries. As is usual with these matters, there is a complicated formula for calculating the exit charge. As a rough guide, the top rate of the exit charge is 4.2%. It is charged on the occasion of the property leaving the trust, although as with chargeable transfers into the trust, it is not immediately due and payable.
- There is a charge levied every ten years, on each ten-year anniversary of the creation of the trust, on all the trust assets over and above the value of the prevailing NRB. Again, a formula is used to determine the charge. Another rough guide is that the ten-year anniversary charge can never exceed 6% of the value of the assets within the trust in excess of the NRB prevailing at the tenth anniversary date. So, for example, if the assets in the trust are worth £1,000 more than the NRB, the charge cannot be greater than £60.

- The nil-rate band available to the trust every ten years is determined by reference to two factors. Firstly, the nil-rate band of the settlor when he created the trust. If he had a full nil-rate band available, the trust will have a full nil-rate band. If he made chargeable transfers within the previous seven years which reduced his nil-rate band at the date the trust was created, the trust will have a nil-rate band reduced to the same extent as his own. The second factor is the value of any chargeable transfers made by the trust (i.e. transfers of property out of the trust) during the ten years prior to the ten-year anniversary. (Note, however, that transfers of property out of the trust in the first ten years are ignored.)
- If a trust is settlor-interested (i.e. if the person who created it can benefit from it in some way, or his wife or civil partner or minor children can take a benefit), there may be a charge on the death of the settlor in addition to the other charges.

The relevant property regime applies to all discretionary trusts created prior to 22 March 2006.

3. Accumulation and maintenance trust IHT regime

As this regime has largely been phased out it will not concern us further.

IHT treatment of lifetime trusts (other than disabled trusts) created on or after 22 March 2006

All lifetime trusts created on or after 22 March 2006 other than disabled trusts are taxed (as far as IHT is concerned) in the same way. They are subject to the 'relevant property' regime (2).

This means that all new lifetime discretionary trusts, life interest trusts and flexible life interest trusts and protective trusts will be taxed as 'relevant property trusts'.

There is no longer a separate 'interest in possession regime' for new lifetime interest in possession trusts; they are taxed under the relevant property regime.

IHT treatment of lifetime trusts for the disabled created on or after 22 March 2006

Transfers into disabled trusts will be PETs subject to the stringent qualifying conditions for such trusts being met. Other aspects of the taxation of such trusts call for specialist advice.

IHT Treatment of other trusts created on death on or after 22 March 2006

IPDI trusts and IHT

IPDI trusts are not subject to the relevant property regime.

1. On death, the death estate is subject to IHT.
2. However, if the person who is given an immediate post-death interest in the death estate is the spouse or civil partner of the deceased, the spouse exemption applies to the trust fund – even though the spouse or civil partner is not in receipt of the trust fund, but only a benefit from the trust fund in the form of an interest in possession.
3. On the death of the life tenant, the value of the trust fund is added to his estate and the total is subject to inheritance tax.

Discretionary trusts and IHT

1. On death, the death estate is subject to IHT.
2. The discretionary trust is then subject to the relevant property regime.

Bare trusts and IHT

Bare trusts are not subject to the relevant property regime. The trust fund of a bare trust is taxed as if it was in the possession and ownership of the individual who is the beneficiary of the trust.

It follows that a lifetime transfer into a bare trust is a PET.

Disabled trusts and IHT

Disabled trusts are not subject to the relevant property regime. A lifetime transfer into such a trust is a PET; there are no exit charges and there is no ten-year charge.

On the death of the disabled person, the value of the trust fund is added to his estate and the total value of the estate plus the trust fund is subject to inheritance tax.

Trusts for bereaved minors/18-25 trusts and IHT

Trusts for bereaved minors, where the minors are to receive their inheritance subject to attaining an age not in excess of 25, receive favourable treatment as compared to relevant property trusts.

There are no ten-year anniversary charges.

If trust property is paid to a beneficiary prior to the age of 18, there will be no exit charge.

If trust property is paid to a beneficiary between the ages of 18 and 25, there will be an exit charge based on the time the trust property has been in the trust since the beneficiary's 18th birthday.

Qualifying interest in possession

Life interest trusts which are not subject to the relevant property tax regime are described as having a 'qualifying interest in possession'.

Life interest trusts created prior to 22 March 2006, transitional serial interests and IPDI trusts all have a qualifying interest in possession

Trusts, IHT and the deemed transfer on death

If a trust is created by the death of an individual, then inheritance tax will be payable in the usual way on the estate of the deceased person because of the deemed transfer on death. Hence a transfer on death into any trust will involve a charge to tax on the fund before it enters the trust.

This will be the case even where the trust is given favourable treatment for IHT purposes, e.g. a disabled trust or a bereaved minor's trust. The favourable treatment will only commence after the assets have entered the trust.

The only cases in which the transfer on death will not cause the trust fund to be subject to a charge to IHT prior to entering the trust are where:

- the transfer on death does not exceed the available NRB; or
- special cases where the trust is a trust for the benefit of an exempt beneficiary – an IPDI trust for a surviving spouse or civil partner, or a trust for a charity. In such a case the spouse exemption or charitable exemption will permit the assets to enter the trust free of inheritance tax because of the exemption.

Qualifying conditions

Note that any trust which is given favourable tax treatment (such as a disabled trust) has to meet a number of qualifying conditions, often a large number of technically demanding qualifying conditions, in order to do so.

A few words about income tax and CGT

The view taken by the previous (Labour) government seemed to be that trusts were undesirable and should be taxed out of existence. Hence the rate of income tax for relevant property trusts was raised to 50%, where it remains. This penal income tax rate can be mitigated by investing in assets which do not produce any income; and/or by paying income to beneficiaries who may then reclaim the tax paid on the trust income, depending on their own financial circumstances.

The rate of CGT is now 28%. Relevant property trusts have the virtue that CGT holdover relief (for an explanation of holdover relief, see section 2.6) can be claimed on assets entering and leaving them.

Summary

The above information is no more than a rough guide to trusts and the current tax treatment of trusts.

It should be noted that it would be possible to write a book bigger than this one devoted purely to the taxation of trusts. It should also be noted that the tax treatment of trusts has seen many changes over the years, particularly recently.

It is highly recommended that if you have any involvement with trusts, you engage the services of an expert – preferably an accountant or solicitor who is experienced with trust work and possibly STEP* qualified.

Conclusion

You might be forgiven for wondering if there is any point to putting assets into trusts given all the taxes!

When they are used as part of a coherent plan and with the benefit of expert advice, trusts can mitigate the impact of inheritance tax and can be useful for maintaining control of family assets after they have been gifted.

It bears repeating that advice is essential when contemplating the use of a trust, and that wills, trust deeds and other legal documents should be professionally drawn up by competent advisors.

1.25 Valuing assets for IHT purposes

This subject is dealt with in Part 4, which in some ways is a more natural home for it than Part 1. Please refer to 4.3 for a discussion of the principles of valuation.

---

*Society of Trust and Estate Practitioners

1.26 Conclusion of Part 1

I would like to draw your attention to the fact that although Part 1 may have seemed to deal with inheritance tax issues in some depth, it is by no means a fully comprehensive guide.

It should be regarded as the minimum required for the general reader to find his or her way around issues that are commonly raised by inheritance tax.

Part 2
Planning During Your Lifetime to Reduce the Burden of Inheritance Tax on Your Death

Is it appropriate for you to plan at all?

Your first consideration should always be yourself. Inheritance tax planning almost invariably involves giving something away, or forgoing something. You should ask yourself whether IHT planning will impact adversely on your lifestyle.

There is a simple approach that you can follow, at least initially, to determine whether it may be appropriate for you to consider any inheritance tax planning.

You will recall from Part 1 that inheritance tax is charged on the transfer of assets at the date of death. You could therefore begin with an assessment of what will happen at the date of your death. If you have read and understood Part 1, this should be (depending on your circumstances) a relatively simple exercise.

As this book is called *Inheritance Tax Made Simple*, guidance is nevertheless provided on how you might proceed.

2.1 Evaluating relevance of tax planning

In order to establish whether inheritance tax planning is relevant to your circumstances you could follow the following steps:

1. calculate your wealth
2. take into account your available nil-rate band (you may need to refer to sections 1.5, 1.6, 1.7, and 1.15 to refresh your memory on this issue)
3. if you are married or a civil partner, consider the impact of the spouse exemption and the transferable nil-rate band of your spouse or civil partner. (If necessary, refer to 1.8, 1.9, 1.10 and 1.15); if you are widowed, then consider the impact of the transferable nil-rate band of your former spouse or CP (as per 1.9 and 1.10).

To make your task even easier, further guidelines are provided below for the most commonly encountered planning situations. Simply identify which situation applies to you, for an instant assessment of your needs.*

If you decide that tax planning is desirable, you should read through the remainder of Part 2 for ideas about what measures (if any) might be appropriate to your circumstances.

2.1.1 Situation 1: a single person who has never married or entered into a civil partnership *or* who is divorced

If you are in this position, then you should have a nil-rate band of £325,000.

Provided that the total value of your money, property and assets does not exceed £325,000, there will be no inheritance tax to pay

---

*The planning situations assume that you have made no lifetime transfers.

Planning Situation 1: a single person who has never married or entered into a CP or who is divorced (2.1.1)

Planning Situation 2: a single person who is a widow or widower or a surviving CP. (2.1.2)

Planning Situation 3: married or in a CP (2.1.3)

Planning Situation 4: single but living with a partner as if married or in a CP (2.1.4)

Planning measures (2.1.5)

on your estate, and probably no requirement to do any inheritance tax planning.

To the extent that your wealth exceeds the figure of £325,000, it will be taxed at the rate of 40%.

2.1.2 Situation 2: a single person who is a widow or widower or a surviving civil partner.

If you are a widow or widower or a surviving CP who has been predeceased by his or her CP, then you should have a nil-rate band of £325,000.

You should also have available the transferable nil-rate band of the spouse or civil partner who has predeceased you, which will amount to a further £325,000. (Provided that your predeceased spouse or civil partner has not used any or all of his or her nil-rate band; and in the case of a predeceased spouse provided that he or she died after 13 March 1975.)

Provided that the total value of your money, property and assets does not exceed £650,000, there will be no inheritance tax to pay on your estate, and probably no requirement to do any inheritance tax planning.

To the extent that your wealth exceeds the figure of £650,000, it will be taxed at 40%.

2.1.3 Situation 3: married or in a CP

You should have a nil-rate band of £325,000.

You ought to take into account the fact that anything you leave to your spouse or civil partner will not suffer inheritance tax due to the spouse exemption, and on the second death the transferable nil-rate band should be available so that the survivor of the married couple or civil partner will be able to leave £650,000 free of tax (2 x nil-rate bands), and to the extent that his or her estate exceeds the sum of £650,000 it will be taxed at 40%.

2.1.4 Situation 4: single but living with a partner as if married or in a civil partnership

There are particular problems facing couples who live as partners but are unmarried and not in a CP.

If one partner dies, leaving his entire estate to the surviving partner, the estates of both partners will be bundled together on the second death, but will have only one nil-rate band available to offset against IHT. (The first nil-rate band will have been used up on the first death, as nil-rate bands can only be transferred between spouses and civil partners.) The result could be an unnecessarily high charge to IHT on the second death.

Examples of how this works in practice, to demonstrate how the high charge to IHT is triggered and how the high charge to IHT might be mitigated, are given in section 2.12.

2.1.5 Planning measures

You are recommended to read all of Part 2, omitting only those sections which clearly do not apply to you – e.g. if you do not have a business, there would be no point in reading the advice about BPR.

If you wish to hone in quickly on measures appropriate to your own circumstances, the following notes may help:

Circumstance	Relevant section
You wish to consider only straightforward planning	2.2
You have an income in excess of your needs	2.2
You wish to make PETs	2.2
You are single and wish to make PETs but there are CGT issues	2.6
You are married/in a CP and wish to make PETs but there are CGT issues	2.5, 2.6, 2.18 (*see* the Planning issues notes to 2.18)
You are unmarried/not in a CP and living as a partner with someone	2.12
You have a business	2.14, 2.15, 2.16, 2.17, 2.18
You have farming property	2.16, 2.17
You occupy a home of substantial value	2.8, 2.9, 2.10, 2.11
You require 'last minute' planning	2.3, 2.13
You wish to use your will to put money into a relevant property trust	2.22

Please be aware that many of the measures will require help from a professional (or at the very least further reading) if you are to implement them successfully.

2.2 Basic tax-planning solutions

The exemptions at the beginning of section 1.16 should have alerted you to the more obvious basic techniques that you can use, which are now covered below.

2.2.1 £3,000 Annual allowance

Make the maximum use of your £3,000 annual allowance. You will recall (1.16.1.1) that you may give away £3,000 per year free of inheritance tax. Remember that if you did not use your £3,000 last year, you can bring it forwards to this year, enabling you to give away £6,000 free of inheritance tax. (Or in the case of a couple who are married or in a CP, and who both give away the maximum available on this basis, £12,000.)

2.2.2 Maintenance of family, normal expenditure out of income, maintenance of dependent relatives

If you consider the £3,000 allowance to be inadequate for your purposes, see whether you can make use of the other lifetime exemptions as well – the small gifts exemption (1.16.1.2), regular payments out of income (1.16.1.3), maintenance of the family (1.16.1.4), maintenance of dependent relatives (1.16.1.4) and gifts in consideration of marriage (1.16.1.5).

2.2.3 PETs

You could also consider PETs if you wish to give away substantial sums of money.

Bear in mind that if you are proposing to give away anything other than money (e.g. a rental property) you will need to explore the CGT implications to ensure that you are not undertaking an exercise that will merely replace one form of tax (IHT) with another (CGT).

You should also remember that if you give away something it must be given away completely so as to qualify as a PET. Generally speaking, if you give something away and continue to make use of it, it will be taxed as part of your estate on death. The classic example of this is the family home. If you were to give away your home to your children and continue to live in it, it would be subject to inheritance tax as if you had never given it away.

The technical term for this is making a "gift with a reservation of benefit" or a GROB. (See 1.20.)

The GROB rule will not apply to every situation where you continue to enjoy a benefit from a gift you have made, but it is probably safe to say that it applies to most gifts.

Note that if you give away a business with the benefit of BPR, you and the recipient will need to be aware of the clawback provisions (see 1.17.2).

2.2.4 PETs via your spouse or civil partner

If you feel that you would like to make a PET but your age and/or medical condition precludes it because you do not expect to survive for the required seven years for the PET to fall out of your estate, you may be able to make the PET if you are fortunate enough to be married to a younger partner, or one in better health.

You could transfer the subject matter of the PET to your spouse or civil partner, at which point no charge to inheritance tax will be triggered because of the spouse exemption. Your spouse or civil partner could then make the PET to the ultimate intended beneficiary, and have a greater chance of making the PET successfully (i.e. tax-free) than you would have made yourself if you had transferred it directly to the intended beneficiary.

2.2.5 Evidence

If you wish to go down any of the above routes – 2.2.1 to 2.2.4 – you should bear in mind that they all potentially raise evidential issues and that at some stage someone may have to provide proof of what you have given away and when it was given. You should, therefore, maintain records and ensure that your gifts qualify for any exemptions and reliefs that you want them to receive. In the case of expenditure out of income, for instance, this means that you need to ensure that the expenditure is demonstrably from income and does not affect your lifestyle, etc.

If you entertain any doubts about your ability to keep records to prove the point, you should take advice on the matter.

2.2.6 Wills

Everyone should make a will, irrespective of any IHT planning considerations. Whether or not you intend to use a will for tax planning purposes, you are advised to make one (see 1.22).

If your estate is taxable, and the residue (or part of it) is to be given to an exempt beneficiary (e.g., a spouse) **consider** making other gifts subject to tax to avoid grossing up (see 4.9.2).

If you are living as a partner with someone but you are unmarried and not in a CP, you face particular problems. It may be possible to address these by means of a will. (2.12).

Those who are wealthy stand to have their estates penalised heavily if they do not make wills (2.21).

2.3 Discounted gift schemes

If you feel that you would like to make a PET but your age and/or medical condition precludes it because you do not expect to survive for the required seven years for the PET to fall out of your estate, you could consider a discounted gift scheme.

The way that such schemes work is rather technical.

They typically involve investing in a bond with an element of life assurance, then gifting the bond into a bare trust (see under 1.24.3 'Types of trust') established at the same time that the investment is made.

The individual who makes the investment takes regular withdrawals from it. The retained right to these regular withdrawals is a right which has a market value.

On establishing the trust, the investor's fund (i.e. that part of the bond which provides for the regular withdrawals) immediately falls outside his estate. The value that is retained in his estate is the market value of the right to the income, which may be worth considerably less than the value of the fund that is required to provide the income.

The remainder of the value of the bond (the proportion which is not providing the income) is treated as a PET, and so may benefit from taper relief if the investor does not survive for seven years after making the gift. After seven years, it should fall outside his estate.

Effectively, these schemes give the investor an immediate reduction in the value of his estate for inheritance tax purposes.

It should be noted that HMRC has not necessarily agreed any IHT reductions with the providers of such schemes, although the basis for calculating the reduction appears to have been agreed in some cases.

They are available through independent financial advisors (IFAs), insurance companies and tied agents* (amongst others).

*A tied agent is an individual who sells financial products offered by only one company, as opposed to an IFA who can sell any of the products that are on the market offered by a wide range of companies. IFAs argue that their service is superior to that of tied agents, on the basis that they can select the best product on the market for each individual case. However, I have known tied agents to argue vociferously that this view is mistaken.

The reduction in inheritance tax will depend on a number of factors, including your age and state of health. If your health is too parlous, it may not be worthwhile entering into such an arrangement. However, you should not make a decision without first taking advice on what the likely reduction would be.

In addition, I would always recommend looking at a number of such schemes from different suppliers rather than just one.

Finally, I have to stress that you will need to take a view on the matter based in the round, not merely on any inheritance tax benefits. A discounted gift scheme is an investment, not merely a vehicle to save tax. If it goes south, any savings may prove illusory as they may be outweighed by investment losses.

2.4 Loan trusts

Loan trusts* are another product supplied by IFAs, insurance companies and tied agents.

The essence of a loan trust is that a trust is set up (usually for the benefit of the client's family) and a sum of money is loaned by the client to the trust.

If you imagine yourself as the client who has entered into a loan trust arrangement using a sum of, say, £200,000, you will appreciate that what will have happened is that you will at this stage be £200,000 the worse off as the £200,000 will be in the trust. However, in theory you will be no worse off, as the trust will owe you the £200,000.

What happens next (or it could happen before the trust is set up) is that the money will be invested in a bond.

*If you have not already done so, please read the section on trusts (1.24) to assist with your understanding of loan trusts. Note that a loan to a trust will be neither a chargeable transfer nor a PET, and nor should it be a GROB. It should be simply (to use a well-worn phrase) what it says on the can: a loan.

The bond will be set up in compliance with current revenue law, which will permit withdrawals of 5% per annum tax free. (Any withdrawal greater than 5% is likely to incur a charge to tax.)

If you take the maximum 5% withdrawal every year, then over a period of 20 years the original loan will be regarded by HMRC as having been paid; the trust will owe you nothing. The bond will have grown within the trust (at least, according to your IFA's projections it probably will have done) and the value of the bond remaining in the trust will pass tax-free to your heirs.

If you find, after entering into a loan trust, some years down the line that you cannot really afford to give away such a large sum of money, you will be able to ask for some of it back, as the loan will be repayable on demand.

This is probably an arrangement suitable only for those for those who anticipate a long and healthy life, as the significant IHT-saving benefits are unlikely to materialise for a number of years. Nevertheless, it may be worth looking into.

As with discounted gift schemes, you will have to take a view on the matter based in the round, not merely on any inheritance tax benefits. A loan trust is an investment, not merely a vehicle to save tax. If it goes belly up, any savings may prove illusory as they could be outweighed by investment losses.

2.5 Making use of the CGT annual exemption of your spouse or civil partner

If you wish to gift an asset that has some taxable gain and would be subject to CGT if you gifted it, and the amount of gain does not exceed (or greatly exceed) double your annual CGT exemption, you may be able to avoid paying CGT by making use of the annual exemption for CGT of your spouse or civil partner.

You could do this by making an initial transfer of a half share in the asset to your spouse or civil partner. This could be done on what is known as a no-gain no-loss basis. A no-gain no-loss basis means that there would be no charge to CGT on the disposal of a half share to your spouse or civil partner. Instead, he or she would receive the half share on the same terms for CGT purposes as you held it. He or she would be credited with the same base value in the asset as you had; and on disposal would be subject to the same tax liability (assuming that he or she had made no other disposals in the same tax year).

Example

Eric wants to give his shares in Really Unlikely Growth Plc to his daughter, Mandy.

The shares were purchased in 2008 for £20,000 and are now valued at £40,000.

The gain is therefore £20,000, which comfortably exceeds Eric's annual exemption of £10,100. If he gives the shares to Mandy as he plans, there will be a liability to CGT of £1,782 (18% tax on the £9,900 over the exemption).

Eric is married to Cecile. If Eric transfers half his shares in Really Unlikely Growth Plc to Cecile, there will be no tax to pay, as they will be transferred to her on a no-gain no-loss basis. She will own shares worth £20,000 and they will be attributed with a base value of £10,000.

Eric now gives his remaining shares in Really Unlikely Growth Plc to Mandy, and Cecile also transfers the shares in the company that she has received from Eric to Mandy.

Both these gifts involve the transfer of shares with a gain of £10,000, and since this is within the annual exemption of £10,100 of both Eric and Cecile, there is no CGT to pay.

2.6 Using trusts to mitigate both CGT and IHT

This section is not a complete guide to the taxation of trusts with regard to CGT. It is merely an outline of how you can use one particular aspect of trusts* and CGT to your advantage to shelter assets from inheritance tax.

You will recall from section 1.18 that gifts of non-cash assets can incur a charge to CGT. (It may be advisable to re-read that section if you have lost track of the details.)

In certain situations, there is a form of relief available where CGT may be charged, known as 'holdover relief'.

The way that holdover relief works is that when you give away an asset that is ripe with gain, you can elect to have the gain and the accompanying CGT charge held over to some future time, to be borne by the recipient of the gift.

Holdover relief is available on gifts made into relevant property trusts.

Example

Sophia has a house which is currently valued at £150,000. She bought it ten years ago for only £80,000. It therefore has a base value of £80,000 and a gain on which she could be taxed of £70,000.

Sophia wants to gift the house to her sons to avoid inheritance tax. However, she is aware that the CGT consequences may outweigh any inheritance tax benefits.

She transfers the house into a relevant property trust that has been set up with her sons as beneficiaries.

Her accountant claims holdover relief on her behalf.

---

*If you have not already done so, I would suggest that you read the section on trusts (1.24) to assist with your understanding of what is involved.

The trust acquires the house with the base value it had when it was disposed of by Sophia, namely £80,000. If and when the trust disposes of the house, it will pay CGT on the gain prevailing at the time of disposal.

If the trust sells the house for £160,000, the gain on which CGT will have to be paid is £160,000 - £80,000 = £80,000.

However, this is not the only option available to the trust. It could in time transfer the house to Sophia's three sons. It could claim holdover relief when it did so, and there would then be no CGT charge to pay on the disposal of the house by the trust.

Sophia's sons would acquire the house with a base value of £80,000. If they sold the house, they would have to pay CGT on the difference between £80,000 and the sale price (assuming that it was sold for full market value).

However, if there were three of them, they would all have annual exemptions of £10,100 available to offset against the charge to CGT. If they were all married, then before selling the house they could all transfer half of their respective shares of the house to their wives. There would then be six annual exemptions available to mitigate the charge to CGT on the sale of the house, amounting to a total of £66,000 of exemption.

If they sold the house for £160,000, the gain would be £80,000. CGT would only be payable on £14,000 of the gain. (£80,000 - £66,000).

Summary

If you wish to transfer assets that are ripe with capital gain, you could consider setting up a trust and transferring the assets into the trust with the benefit of holdover relief.

Planning issues

- Holdover relief should be available on the assets both on entering the trust and on leaving it.
- Married beneficiaries and those in civil partnership could take advantage of the annual CGT allowance of their spouses or civil partners when disposing of the assets.
- There are time limits on claiming holdover relief and it must be claimed by both parties (transferor and transferee).

A reminder

If you make a transfer (i.e. for most practical purposes a gift) into a relevant property trust, it will be a chargeable transfer. This means that it will be immediately chargeable to inheritance tax. This in turn means that any gift that you make into a trust should amount to less than your nil-rate band of (in 2010) £325,000 (if you have made no previous transfers), so as to be tax-free. You should only make transfers greater than this subject to taking advice on a coherent tax-planning strategy.

In fact any transfer into a relevant property trust probably calls for advice.

2.7 Sale and purchase of smaller replacement home

If you occupy a house that is too big for your needs, you could consider (if you can put up with the upheaval) selling your house and downsizing. Any surplus money from the sale of your home and purchase of a replacement property could be given away, possibly as a PET.

2.8 Gifting part of your home

Generally, if you give your home to someone and continue to occupy the home, there will be no benefit as far as inheritance tax is concerned. The gift will be classified by HMRC as a GROB and taxed as part of your estate on death (see 1.18).

However, it is possible to give away a share in your home and continue to occupy it, and reduce the value of the home for the purposes of inheritance tax.

Example

Tom lives on his own in a large house. Given the value of his house and the other assets in his estate, there will be a charge to inheritance tax on his death.

He gives away a half share in the house to his daughter Sandra, who moves in and occupies the house with him.

The gift of the share in the house to Sandra is treated as a PET, notwithstanding that the GROB rules and/or pre-owned assets charge would appear to apply. This particular transaction is exempt from the GROB rules and the pre-owned assets charge.

The exemption applies if the donor:

- makes a gift of an *undivided* share of an interest in land; and
- the donor shares occupation of the land with the recipient; and
- the donor does not receive any benefit provided by or at the expense of the recipient in some way connected with the gift.

A gift of the whole property or (for example) a lease will not be exempt as what is given away must be an "undivided share".

The donor must pay his share of all the running costs of the house, otherwise he would be receiving a "benefit provided by or at the expense of the recipient in some way connected with the gift". (Inasmuch as the recipient would be paying some proportion of the running costs that should be rightly borne by the donor.)

The running costs are of two types: those connected with maintenance and those connected with occupation (utility bills, etc).

The bills connected with maintenance should be paid by the owning parties on the basis of their respective shares in the property. E.g. if the donor owned 60%, he should pay 60% of any roof repairs, etc.

The bills connected with maintenance could be paid on the basis of occupation – e.g. if the donor occupied less of the property than the recipient, he could pay proportionately less of the utility bills, etc.

In theory a homeowner could give away a large proportion of his house – say up to 99% – on this basis and have the liability to a charge to inheritance tax on his home eliminated. In practice, overly aggressive tax planning is probably better avoided because it is likely to be challenged by HMRC; a gift of over 80% might well come to grief as a result of such a challenge. The challenge, if there was one, would arise at a stage when it would be too late to unravel the arrangement – on the death of the homeowner. The submission of the tax forms to HMRC detailing his estate on death would be the trigger. (When an individual dies, his personal representatives must prepare and submit details of the estate to the probate registry or to HMRC when applying for probate. The information requested in the official forms on which the details are submitted would alert HMRC to the circumstances of the homeowners and the extent of the gift of the home.)

Early advice on this is required from an expert, and meticulous record keeping with regard to bill paying is advisable.

2.9 Severing and gifting part of your home

If there is part of your home that you do not have to use, it may be possible to give away that part and continue to occupy the remainder of your home.

In order to avoid falling foul of the GROB rules, the part of your home that you give away should preferably be physically separated in some way from your main residence. E.g. a separate annex would be ideal. In any event, always take advice on whether your proposal would pass muster with HMRC and have the land properly conveyed to the beneficiary who is to be the new owner.

The conveyancing should be carried out by someone suitably qualified – a solicitor or licensed conveyancer. The tax advice would probably require a solicitor or accountant.

2.10 Commercial arrangements and the family home

As previously noted, gifting the family home is fraught with difficulties due to the rules on associated operations, and the GROB and POAT rules (see 1.20 and 1.21).

Notwithstanding these rules, it is possible to gift the value of your home, or to reduce the value of your home in your estate, and continue to occupy it, provided that you are well advised.

The key to gifting your house and continuing to occupy it, without falling foul of the GROB and POAT rules, is to retain your right to occupy it via a commercial arrangement. A commercial arrangement in this context means that you would pay for the privilege of occupying your former home, in the same way as you would pay to occupy it if you were renting it from someone – and you would pay the same amount. The same amount would be the rent that would be paid if the house was rented out on the open market to tenants willing to pay the full market value rent.

You would have to ensure that your commercial arrangement was entered into by means of:

- a transaction at arm's length (i.e., one in which the buyer and seller act independently of one another in their own self interest) with a person not connected with you; or
- a transaction such as might be expected to be made at arm's length by persons not connected with each other.

Tax advisors may be able to advise you of a number of possibilities.

One example of such a transaction might be to create a lease in your home in your own favour, then sell the freehold at a market value.

Freehold means that you own the home with the most complete form of ownership. There is no owner above you with a superior claim to the home.

Leasehold is regarded as a lesser form of ownership than freehold. If a home is held subject to a lease, it means that at some stage the person with the freehold has granted a right to someone else (the leaseholder) to use the home. This right will come at a price, usually in the form of a rent. The leaseholder has a person with a superior form of ownership above him – the freeholder. The lease will have a time limit, which means that at some stage the lease would expire, and possession of the home would revert to the freeholder.

Another distinction is that a freeholder can do what he wants to with his freehold home (within reason!) but a leaseholder may find that his actions in respect of his home are limited by the terms of the lease.

There are many types of lease and they can run for many time periods. It is quite common for flats and apartments to be held on a 99-year lease.

Some leasehold property can be sold in the same way as freehold property; however, there are implications for the sale price if the lease is a short one.

For instance, with a 99-year lease on a flat, the sale value of the leasehold tends to decline. The right to occupy a flat for ten years would generally be worth less than the right to occupy it for 99 years.

Some leases are tantamount to freehold ownership – there are many 999-year leases.

In order for this arrangement to work (i.e. to be effective in reducing the liability of your estate to inheritance tax), the rent paid must be a market value rent. A rent at below market value would amount to a reservation of a benefit of some kind. A reservation of benefit would trigger the GROB rules, with the result that there would be no mitigation of IHT and quite possibly a greater sum to pay than if the arrangement had not been entered into (1.24).

If you intend to enter into such an arrangement, you have to treat the exercise of determining the rent and the terms of the lease in the same way that you would treat a wholly commercial transaction. The lease and rent paid should be the same as would be arrived at by two parties negotiating at arm's length. This implies the involvement of professionals to ascertain a market value rent as well as in the drawing up of the lease, arranging the sale of the freehold and providing tax advice.

Note that the main residence exemption for CGT purposes would be lost and that stamp duty would be payable on the sale.

2.11 Gift and leaseback of the family home

The GROB rules do not apply to the home if you give it away and occupy it subject to paying rent at the full market value.

You could, therefore, give away your home, continue to occupy it and have the gift treated as a PET, provided that you agreed to pay rent to the new owner(s).

You would have to treat the arrangement as if it were a commercial transaction. This would involve taking professional advice on the level of rent to be paid, terms of occupation, etc.

The arrangement would have to be fully documented and any failure to comply with the 'market value' requirement would result in the gift being treated as a gift with a reservation of benefit, and lead to possibly onerous tax consequences.

Note that the main residence relief for CGT purposes (1.18) would be lost if you were to enter into such an arrangement.

2.12 Will arrangements for couples living as partners

This section addresses the very specific needs of those couples who are living as partners but are unmarried and not in a civil partnership.

If one partner dies, leaving his entire estate to the surviving partner, the estates of both partners will be bundled together on the second death, but will have only one nil-rate band available to offset against IHT. (The first nil-rate band will have been used up on the first death, as nil-rate bands can only be transferred between spouses and CP.) The result could be an unnecessarily high charge to IHT on the second death.

Example 1

Ted and Joyce are an unmarried couple who own money, property and assets amounting to £350,000 each. Ted dies first, having made a will which gives everything he owns to Joyce. She now owns an estate worth £700,000.

When Joyce dies, leaving her estate to their son Jack, the inheritance tax bill is £150,000:

£700,000

Less Joyce's nil-rate band of (£325,000)

£375,000

£375,000 x 40% = £150,000

If Joyce had been married to Ted, the inheritance tax bill would have been only £20,000:

£700,000

Less Joyce's nil-rate band of £325,000

And less Ted's nil-rate band of £325,000

(£650,000)

£50,000

£50,000 x 40% = £20,000

Gift of nil-rate band to a third party

In Example 1, above, Ted and Joyce could improve on the situation by arranging to leave some or all of their assets to Charles on the first death.

The way that this could be done would be for Ted to make a will which says something along the lines of:

> *"I give a sum equal to the value of my nil-rate band at death to my son Jack and I give the residue (1.22.4) to my partner Joyce."*

Similarly, Joyce would make a will which would say something along the lines of:

> *"I give a sum equal to the value of my nil-rate band at death to my son Jack and I give the residue to my partner Ted."*

Example 2

Ted dies first. His will gives his available nil-rate band of £325,000 to Jack, the son he has with Joyce. The inheritance tax bill is £10,000.

(Ted's estate of £350,000 less his nil-rate band of £325,000, leaves a figure of £25,000, which will be subject to IHT at 40%, giving rise to a £10,000 charge to tax.)

When Joyce dies, leaving her estate to their son, the tax bill is again £10,000. In other words, for each estate of £350,000:

£350,000
Less the nil-rate band of (£325,000)
£25,000
£25,000 x 40% = £10,000

Note that the total IHT payable is £20,000, as compared with an IHT bill of £150,000 if Ted had left everything to Joyce. (See previous example.)

Obviously this approach will only work if the finances of the couple are such that it can be said with certainty that the surviving partner will not need access to the funds of the first to die which have been gifted to the third party

Gift into nil-rate band discretionary trust with power to make loans to survivor

This approach may be taken where there is a possibility that the surviving partner may need to use funds provided by the first to die. It has the merit that it permits the use of funds by the survivor, while maintaining the full value of the nil-rate band of both partners.

The scheme can be implemented by both partners making wills which incorporate a discretionary trust. The discretionary trust would have a number of beneficiaries, one of whom would be the surviving partner.

Both wills would contain a gift of the value of the nil-rate band to be paid into the discretionary trust (e.g. "I give the sum of £325,000 to be held in the following trust..." or "I give a sum equal to the value of the nil-rate band at the date of my death to be held in the following trusts...")

The residue would in most cases be left to the surviving partner (e.g. "I give the residue of my estate to my partner Joyce...")

The surviving partner could, if needs be, take loans from the discretionary trust.

On the death of the surviving partner, the loans would be called in by the trust and would reduce the value of the estate of the survivor.

Example 3

This is a reprise of the original example using Ted and Joyce.

Ted and Joyce are an unmarried couple who own money, property and assets amounting to £350,000 each. Ted dies first, having made a will which makes a tax-free gift of his money, property and assets up to the value of his nil-rate band into a discretionary trust. His will gives everything in excess of the value of his nil-rate band to Joyce.

So the situation on Ted's death is as follows:

Estate: £350,000

Nil-rate band RB trust: £325,000

Inheritance tax: £10,000 (This is the tax on the £25,000 above the £325,000 left to Joyce)

Joyce: £15,000 (i.e. £25,000 less the £10,000 tax bill).

Joyce has £350,000 herself, but this is all tied up in the house she lives in. Over the years she borrows £40,000 from the trust to get by.

On Joyce's death, she has left a will leaving her entire estate to Jack, the son she had with Ted.

Her estate is comprised of a house worth £350,000, but she owes £40,000 (to the trust) so her net estate (after taking into account the £40,000 debt) is only £310,000. There is therefore no IHT to pay on Joyce's estate.

The house is sold and the loan of £40,000 is called in by the trust.

The remaining sale proceeds of £310,000 are given to Jack.

The trust has a trust fund of £325,000* which is given free of IHT to Jack.

Jack has received an estate worth a total of £635,000 and on which the IHT bill has been only £10,000.

The tax planning arrangements did not denude Joyce of funds, as she was assisted with her financial needs during her lifetime.

Gift into nil-rate band discretionary trust with charge scheme

In some cases substantial amounts of the wealth of the couple may be tied up in their home, and it may not be feasible to siphon a large sum of money into a trust. In such cases a modified version of the scheme using the nil-rate band trust may be appropriate.

Once again, the charge scheme can be implemented by both partners making wills which incorporate a discretionary trust. Once again, the discretionary trust would have a number of beneficiaries, one of whom would be the surviving partner.

Both wills would contain a gift of the value of the nil-rate band to be paid into the discretionary trust (e.g. "I give the sum of £325,000 to be held on the following trust..." or "I give a sum equal to the value of the nil-rate band at the date of my death to be held on the following trusts...").

The residue would, in most cases, be left to the surviving partner.

The wills would state that the nil-rate band gift could be satisfied by means of a charge on the family home.

On the death of the surviving partner, the home would be sold and the charge would be paid from the sale proceeds.

The result for tax purposes should be similar to that shown in the preceding example in which Ted's will incorporated a discretionary trust.

*Originally the trust fund amounted to £325,000. The trust made loans of £40,000 to Joyce, reducing the trust fund to £285,000. The £40,000 in loans was repaid from Joyce's estate on her death, bringing the trust fund back up to £325,000.

Planning issues

- In order to comply with trust laws, any loan made by the trust might have to include a provision for interest of some kind. This could be a provision that any outstanding balance on the loan would be index linked. (Tax laws might be satisfied by an interest-free loan.)
- Income tax would be payable on the interest charged. (In some cases interest might not be charged. Instead, the arrangement might be for the debt to be index linked, which would mean that it would appreciate in line with the Retail Price Index or the Consumer Price Index. If this arrangement were to be made, CGT might be payable on the rise in value of the outstanding loan, rather than income tax.)
- The loan or charge would probably have to be repayable on demand, although in practice it would probably remain outstanding until the death of the surviving partner.
- HMRC would not permit the debt or charge to be deducted from the estate for IHT purposes if it were seen to be a sham. The trustees would therefore have to have evidence that they were actively managing the trust and actively considering calling in the loan/charge from time to time. This would require regular meetings (probably at least once a year) to discuss trust matters, including considering calling in the loan. The discussions would have to be minuted.
- It might help if, on one occasion at least, the opinion of a barrister were to be sought on the legalities and practicalities of calling in the outstanding debt/charge.
- If the charge scheme was being used and the house was jointly owned it would have to be owned by the partners as tenants in common. This might involve severing the tenancy (1.23).

2.13 Business property: AIM/USM shares

You may recall that unquoted shares in a trading company qualify for BPR of 100%. Unquoted shares (for the purposes of BPR) include shares which are traded in the Unlisted Securities Market (USM shares) or the Alternative Investment Market (AIM shares).

This means that one route to obtaining 100% relief from inheritance tax on some of your money would be to use it to buy USM shares or AIM shares.

There are a number of factors and pitfalls that you need to be wary of:

- in order for the shares to qualify for the relief, you will need to own them for two years
- the companies represented by the shares will have to be qualifying companies, not (e.g.) investment companies
- you will need to bear in mind the volatility of the stock market. The tax benefits could be wiped out if there is a significant fall in the value of your AIM portfolio.

The shares will not qualify for BPR if they are traded on a recognised overseas stock exchange. Some AIM and USM shares are also traded overseas and as a result do not qualify for BPR.

Because of the potential volatility of your investment, and the need to identify shares which qualify for BPR (i.e. are not traded on recognised overseas exchanges as well as the AIM and USM), you need seriously good advice. It may also be a requirement that you should not be too risk averse.

2.14 Sheltering assets in the family business

If you own or control a company, it may be possible to make use of the business as a vehicle for inheritance tax planning.

The business must be one which would qualify for BPR (see 1.17.1). For example, if the business is a limited company and could make use of new capital, you could arrange an injection of capital into the company in exchange for shares which would (subject to the BPR qualifying factors) qualify for BPR.

Note that the company would have to be able to make use of the capital – money lying dormant in a bank account would not qualify for BPR and would not assist matters.

The usual cautions regarding investments of any kind would apply – you would have to be confident about the stability of the business and so on.

2.15 Converting 50% BPR to 100% BPR

Certain business assets qualify for BPR of only 50% (see 1.17.1). For example: land, buildings, machinery or plants used by a company controlled by the transferor or by a partnership of which the transferor was a member.

If you own land, buildings, machinery or a plant which is used by a company that you control or a partnership of which you are a member, the transfer of the land, buildings, machinery or plant to the company or partnership could raise the BPR available on the asset from 50% to 100%.

This is because BPR on land, buildings, machinery or plants used by a company, controlled by the transferor, is given at 50% (1.17.1); whereas unquoted shares in a company, partnership interests, and quoted shares which confer control of the company on the transferor, attract the relief at 100%.

So if you own a plant used by your limited company, the plant may qualify for BPR of 50%. If the same plant is owned by your limited company rather than by you, you will own shares in the company that owns the plant, and the shares will qualify for 100% BPR (subject to meeting the qualifying conditions).

Hence the transfer of the plant to the company will effectively increase the 50% relief to 100% relief.

Remember that a straight transfer of land, buildings, machinery or plant to the company would be a chargeable transfer. So the transfer would probably have to be by means of the company exchanging shares for the assets that were transferred, in order to make the most of the tax benefits.

Consideration would have to be given to CGT issues. Holdover relief might be available to defer any charge to CGT.

2.16 Maximising BPR and APR by allocating debts to non-business and non-agricultural assets

If you have a company which qualifies for BPR and you have borrowed money to finance the business, the debt will in the normal course of events be deducted from the value of the company*, driving down the BPR available to your estate.

If, however, the debt is secured against a non-business asset, the effect may be to reduce the value of the non-business asset** rather than the value of the business itself, preserving the value of the business and so maximising the BPR available to your estate.

With agricultural property, liabilities are only deducted from the value of the agricultural property if they are charged against it***.

---

*"(a) the value of a business or of an interest in a business shall be taken to be its net value;

"(b) the net value of a business is the value of the assets used in the business (including goodwill) reduced by the aggregate amount of any liabilities incurred for the purposes of the business;

"(c) in ascertaining the net value of an interest in a business, no regard shall be had to assets or liabilities other than those by reference to which the net value of the entire business would fall to be ascertained" (IHTA 1984 s110)

**A liability which is an encumbrance on any property shall, so far as possible, be taken to reduce the value of that property. (IHTA 1984 s162(4))

***A charge is essentially a mortgage. If a debt is charged against a property, then on the sale of that property the sale proceeds must be used to pay the debt in priority to anything else.

This suggests that if a farm requires finance, any loan should, if possible, not be secured against the agricultural property, and (again, if at all possible) secured against some other asset in the estate.

2.17 Maximising BPR and APR – the double-dip will

A business valued at £300,000 may be used to extract £600,000 worth of value tax-free from an estate if the business owner is well advised. This may be achieved by using a double-dip will (as it is often referred to).

The concept behind this kind of will is essentially quite simple. Nevertheless, you may have to read this section a number of times to fully grasp the idea.

It is best explained by way of an example.

Example

Jed is married to Sandra. He has a business valued at £300,000, and cash assets of £1,000,000. Sandra is wealthy in her own right.

They have two adult children, Jack and Marilyn.

Jed sets up two lifetime discretionary trusts on different days, Trust 1 and Trust 2, in each of which there is only the nominal sum of £10 cash.

He makes a will in which he leaves a sum of money amounting to his nil-rate band of £325,000 into Trust 1, and all his business property into Trust 2.

He leaves the rest of his estate to his wife Sandra.

When Jed dies (conveniently prior to Sandra) his nil-rate band is paid as per his will into Trust 1.

This exhausts Jed's nil-rate band. This means that any other transfers from Jed's estate will be chargeable unless reliefs or exemptions apply to them.

We know that that the transfer to Sandra is exempt, as she receives the benefit of the spouse exemption.

That leaves the transfer of Jed's business to Trust 2.

Since Jed's nil-rate band has been used up, HMRC will have to make an immediate determination as to whether the business should be given BPR.

If the business does get full BPR of 100% on its entire value of £300,000, it can be transferred to the trust without incurring any charges to inheritance tax.

The situation at this point is that:

- Trust 1 contains the sum of £325,000
- Trust 2 contains the business, valued at £300,000.

Sandra can buy the business from Trust 2 for £300,000, and as this is a transfer for the market value, as if at arm's length, there will be no inheritance tax payable on the transaction.

After Sandra has owned the business for two years, it will qualify as business property in her hands and will qualify for BPR. On her death, all going well, the business will still get for 100% BPR.

A total of £1,250,000 in value will have left Jed's and Sandra's estate tax free; £300,000 courtesy of BPR on Jed's death (represented by the £300,000 used to buy the business) and a further £325,000 courtesy of his nil-rate band; then £300,000 on Sandra's death in the form of the business given BPR at 100% and a further £325,000 due to Sandra's nil-rate band.

Planning issues

- Although the example refers to BPR, it would, of course, be possible to use this scheme in conjunction with APR.
- If the business had not been given 100% BPR, it could have been appointed back out of the trust to Sandra. Provided that this was done more than three months after Jed's death, but less than two years after it, it would be treated as a disposition by his will and there would be no liability to IHT because of the spouse exemption.
- The option to appoint back to the surviving spouse is particularly useful if there is any doubt about the availability of BPR. Indeed, there is a case to be made that every business owner with a business of significant value who is married or in a civil partnership should make a will incorporating these provisions to enable planning measures to be taken in the event that BPR is denied.
- There would possibly be CGT issues (1.18) to consider on the sale of the business to the surviving spouse or civil partner. In addition there could be stamp duty issues. Stamp duty is a tax on documents, and the documents required to transfer the company could give rise to a charge to the duty.
- The couple must die in the right order, as it were, (the owner of the business first), and the surviving spouse or civil partner must survive the sale of the business by at least the two years required to obtain BPR.

2.18 The 'Family Debt Scheme'

This is one of the very rare situations where it may be possible to have your cake and eat it, i.e. to dispose of an asset and continue to derive some benefit from it. Unfortunately it is only available in a limited set of circumstances.

The situation in which it can be utilised is that in which one party of a marriage or civil partnership has an income-producing asset in his or her own name which would be subject to inheritance tax on death. (Unless left to the surviving spouse or civil partner, of course, in which case it would be subject to inheritance tax on the second death – it takes advantage of the spouse exception). A good example of this would probably be shares in a property company. (Note that this is only an example and is not intended to imply that the use of the scheme is restricted to property companies).

If we assume that the husband of a married couple has a limited company worth £2,000,000, and he owns all the shares issued by the company, he could have an arrangement with his wife that she would buy the shares from him for the market value of £2,000,000. She would then own the company.

The purchase would not be funded by cash, but by a debt. The wife would finance the purchase of the shares by means of a loan given to her by her husband.

No money would change hands; the transaction would take place and afterwards the wife would be the registered owner of the shares, while the husband would have documents to prove that his wife owed him £2,000,000.

The husband would give away the debt – probably to the child or children of the married couple.

The end result of the two transactions would be that the wife would own the shares worth £2,000,000 and would owe her children the sum of £2,000,000.

The husband would have made a PET to the value of £2,000,000.

Provided that the husband survived the PET by the period of seven years, it would not be cumulated (1.15.6) with his estate on death.

On the wife's death, the shares worth in the region of £2,000,000 would be in her estate. However, she would owe the sum of £2,000,000 to her children, which would more than likely cover the value of all or most of the shareholding.

The beauty of the scheme is that the wife can continue to derive the income from the shares. If it had been given away as a PET, the couple would have entirely lost the benefits of the income.

Planning issues

- The initial sale of the shares to the wife could possibly trigger a charge to CGT if it were made to anyone else. Transfers of assets between spouses and CPs do not attract a charge to CGT. (They are transferred on what is referred to as a 'no-gain no-loss basis'. This means that the transferee receives them with the same base value that they had while owned by the transferor.)
- There would be stamp duty to pay on the value of the shares at the rate of 0.5%, resulting in a charge of £10,000. This may sound like a high charge, but compared to the 40% rate of inheritance tax is something of a bargain.
- If the assets were not shares in, say, a property company, but rental properties held by the husband, the stamp duty would be at the rate of 5%.
- This is not a scheme to be entered into on the basis of homemade documents. You will need expert legal advice, and even experienced solicitors will probably have the documentation drawn up by counsel.
- The family debt scheme may be appropriate wherever there is an asset which is ripe with capital gain, (1.18) even if the asset is not income producing.

2.19 Using trusts to mitigate IHT – three approaches

There are at least three approaches available to mitigate IHT using lifetime trusts.

2.19.1 Transfers within your nil-rate band

As previously noted, most transfers into lifetime trusts will be chargeable transfers.

This implies that each and every transfer into a trust could potentially trigger a charge to inheritance tax. However, you can transfer money into a trust without incurring IHT if you do so using an amount of money which falls within your available nil-rate band.

Provided you survive the transfer for a period of seven years, it will not incur a charge to inheritance tax. You will then be able to repeat the trick. You may be able to put in excess of £1,000,000 into trust in this way without incurring a charge to IHT (see 1.5 and 2.2.20).

Example

If you have not used up any of your nil-rate band, you will have an NRB available of £325,000. If you transfer £325,000 there will not be any charge to inheritance tax as the transfer will fall within your nil-rate band. Repeat in seven years time.

2.19.2 Transfers in excess of your nil-rate band

You could take the view that it is worth losing 20% of the value of your assets to IHT now rather than losing 40% later (on death!).

If you take this view, then transfers of money, property and assets in excess of the nil-rate band into lifetime trusts are worth considering.

2.19.3 Transfers into disabled trusts

If there is an individual who is disabled, to whom you wish to leave any of your estate, you could consider setting up a form of trust for that person known as a disabled trust. A transfer into that trust would then be a PET rather than a chargeable transfer.

Note that there is a very specific and lengthy definition of what constitutes a disabled person for these purposes. You will need to take advice on whether the individual you wish to benefit qualifies as a disabled person for these particular tax purposes.

Although such a transfer will be a PET, it may not eliminate IHT altogether, even if you survive the transfer by seven years. On the death of the disabled person, the value of the trust assets will be added to the value of the disabled person's estate and the total amount will then be subject to inheritance tax.

2.20 Life insurance

If gifting property is not an option to reduce inheritance tax liability, you could consider insuring against the liability.

Life policies may be particularly useful if you have made a PET, as you may be able to insure against the possibility of failing to survive for the required period. The drawback to taking out a policy of life insurance to pay such IHT is that the life policy itself could increase the liability to IHT if the proceeds are payable to the estate of the insured.

The purpose for which you take out a policy of life insurance is immaterial, as far as the IHT consequences are concerned. If the proceeds of the policy are payable to your estate on death, they will be added to your estate on death, and subject to inheritance tax along with all your other assets.

This drawback can be eliminated if the policy is written in trust, so that the proceeds are payable to the trust rather than the estate of the insured party. The insured must not be a beneficiary of the trust.

The policy must be put in trust when it commences, otherwise the transfer of the policy might give rise to a tax charge on the basis that the transfer is a gift and the policy has a value.

Payments of the premiums should be treated as normal expenditure out of income, subject to compliance with the criteria for such treatment.

IFAs should be able to advise on suitable policies and provide off-the-shelf trusts to receive the proceeds.

2.21 Making wills – a must for everyone and in particular for the wealthy

Wills are important for everyone, but for very wealthy couples who are married or in a civil partnership they can have particular importance in avoiding inheritance tax charges on the first death.

The following example should serve to explain why.

Example

Alex and Frieda are young and wealthy. They each have assets totalling £3 million. They have two young children who are both minors, aged five and seven.

Frieda unexpectedly dies without having made a will.

Under the rules of intestacy (the rules that take effect and govern the distribution of an estate when there is no will), the estate is distributed as follows:

> Alex receives the sum of £250,000* and Frieda's personal chattels (these are the moveable possessions owned by Frieda).

*This is known as the 'statutory legacy'. The statutory legacy changes from time to time. It became £250,000 on 1 February 2009, in cases where there was a surviving spouse and children. Prior to that date it was £125,000. It was last changed (to £125,000) in 1993. There appears to be no mechanism for regular changes to increase the statutory legacy regularly (say, in line with inflation), although such mechanisms have been considered (Department for Constitutional Affairs Consultation Paper CP 11/05 'Administration of Estates – review of Statutory Legacy').

He is given a life interest (see 1.24.2) in half the residue, and the remaining half of the residue is held in trust for the children when they become 18 years old.

The tax repercussions are as follows:

The £250,000 and the chattels are free of IHT due to the spouse exemption.

The life interest is also free of IHT due to the spouse exemption (it is an IPDI trust – see 1.24.3, page 85).

The half share in the residue given to the children suffers a swinging £420,000 charge to tax:

	£
Share in residue left to the children:	1,375,000
Less: Frieda's NRB:	(325,000)
Taxable estate:	1,050,000
	£1,050,000 @ 40% = £420,000

If Frieda had made a will leaving most of her estate to Alex (i.e., to the extent that not more than the value of her nil rate band was given to other beneficiaries) there would have been no IHT payable because of the spouse exemption. Alex might have then been in a position to plan to mitigate the estate given to the children by making use of PETs (1.15).*

2.22 Directing property into trusts when making wills (pilot trusts)

This is not a method of reducing the amount of IHT payable on your estate. It is a means by which you can minimise the amount

*See also 1.12.3. which advises on maximising the tax savings with wills when a husband or wife has the benefit of a transferable NRB from a prior marriage.

of IHT that will be paid if you direct your estate (or part of your estate) into a relevant property trust (1.24.3).

You will recall from 1.24.3 that relevant property trusts are taxed every ten years, and that the charge to tax is based on the value of the trust assets over and above the value of the nil-rate band.

If a testator is proposing to leave assets into such a trust by means of his will, the ten-year charge to IHT can be reduced, or avoided altogether, if a certain amount of forward planning is undertaken.

During his lifetime the testator could create two or more relevant property trusts using a sum of only ten pounds or so as the trust fund for each of the trusts.

The testator's will could then be drafted so as to direct (say) 1/3 of his estate into each of the three different trusts of this kind created during his lifetime.

Each trust would have its own nil-rate band, which would mean that IHT would only become an issue on the ten-year anniversary if the value of the assets in trust exceeded the value of three nil-rate bands, as opposed to the value of one nil-rate band. (£975,000 as opposed to £325,000.)

There would potentially be a problem with the burden of administrative costs – the need for three sets of accounts and tax returns, and so on. However, this could be addressed by merging the three trusts into one single trust after the death of the testator. The single trust would still be treated for IHT purposes as three trusts with three nil-rate bands. (IHTA 1984 s81.)

Note that:

- The trusts would have to be created on different days. Otherwise the tax benefits would not be available.
- The trusts would have to be in existence before the will was made.

2.23 Seemingly clever strategies to avoid, as they do not work

This section serves as a reminder about planning solutions to be *avoided*.

Making a modest transfer to bring about a large reduction to the estate

If you are of an ingenious turn of mind, you may have read the first section ('IHT in a nutshell' – 1.2) and worked out that, as inheritance tax is charged on transfers of value, you could find ways of considerably reducing the value of your estate without making a considerable transfer of value.

Example

An oft-used example is one where George gives his son Michael (for example) a chair from a set of four Chippendale chairs. Together as a set, the chairs are worth £50,000, but individually any chairs that are not part of an entire set are worth only £2,000 each. So by giving Michael a chair, George has reduced the value of his estate by £44,000 (i.e. £50,000, less £2,000 of one chair, and with the three remaining ones only worth £2,000 each). He has given away only £2,000 to Michael, which means that only £2,000 will be added to his cumulative total should he die in the next seven years. It seems like a good wheeze.

Unfortunately the transfer of value is based on the *loss to the transferor's estate*. The loss caused by the gift of the chair to Michael is £44,000, and that is therefore the value which has been transferred – even though the one chair has a market value of only £2,000.

Gifts with a reservation of benefit

You could consider transferring your residence (i.e. the home that you live in) to your children, while continuing to live in it. Unfortunately this will not bring about the desired effect.

If you give away an asset and continue to treat it as your own, or fail to fully give up possession of it, the asset will be treated as part of your estate on death. The technical term for such a gift is a 'gift with a reservation of benefit', or a 'GROB' (1.20).

There would actually be a potential *disadvantage* in tax terms in transferring your residence to your children; you would lose the main residence relief for capital gains tax purposes, with the result that if your house gained in value significantly, and you wanted to sell it, you could end up paying tax on the proceeds of sale.

You might think that the main residence relief would pass to your children – but it would not do so if you gave them the house and continued to occupy it, while they occupied their own home elsewhere. Main residence relief applies only in respect of your main residence. For these purposes, your main residence is a home in which you genuinely live on a regular basis for at least some of the time.

If your children actually did occupy the house with you on a regular basis, then subject to giving notice to HMRC in the required form at the required time, they could claim main residence relief if the house were to be sold. However, for inheritance tax purposes the gift of the house would still be a GROB.

There are valid approaches you can use, even in conjunction with the family home, which avoid the GROB rules – please read preceding sections 2.7, 2.8, 2.9, 2.10 and 2.11.

Sheltering assets within your company

This is an option that can work (see above: 2.15) but it all depends on the approach taken.

You may have a company which will attract business property relief and be tempted to retain a plot of land in the company, or a large sum of money in a company bank account, indefinitely, in the expectation that one day (e.g. on your death) these assets will be treated as company assets and receive the benefit of business property relief (1.17.1).

However, unless your personal representatives can demonstrate that the parcel of land or sum of money are used in the conduct of your business, and not merely lying idle, the prospects for business property relief on these assets are slim to non-existent.

If you simply give your company a bung, this will be a chargeable transfer. To add insult to injury, it will not even receive the benefit of BPR after it has entered the company – not unless it can be shown that it is used by the company for business purposes.

2.24 Conclusion to Part 2

The above catalogue of IHT planning methods is not necessarily comprehensive; there may be other approaches that you can take.

If you intend to carry out any inheritance tax planning, it may be advisable to consult an accountant, a solicitor and an IFA. They will all have their own approaches to your problem and may be able to provide you with different solutions to choose from. Moreover, one advisor, however well informed, is unlikely to have all the answers to every IHT question that you could possibly put to him or her.

A general piece of advice that may be appropriate to everyone is to keep it simple as far as is practicably possible. You should consider all the most basic methods of inheritance tax planning, and it is only when you have exhausted these, or ruled them out for some reason, that you should move on to the more exotic methods.

Part 3
Reducing the Burden of IHT on an Inheritance

Preamble

This section is intended to assist those who are receiving an inheritance from someone who has died which will be subject to inheritance tax before they receive it. Advice should probably be sought as soon as possible if you are in this position, as your options to do anything about it generally cease two years after the date of death. This is, simply, because the most effective of the planning measures at your disposal can only be used within two years of the date of death.

There may be two different sets of people involved in this situation: the beneficiaries of an estate (the ones who will receive an inheritance), and the personal representatives (the individuals responsible for administering the estate and giving the beneficiaries their inherited wealth).

Sometimes an individual may be a personal representative and a beneficiary at one and the same time. That is, he or she may have the task of administering an estate, and may also be inheriting some or all of the estate.

The issue of who is a beneficiary and who is a personal representative with regard to tax mitigation can be important, as there are tax mitigation options that are the province of the personal representatives and cannot be exercised by the beneficiaries, and there are tax mitigation options that are the province of the beneficiaries and cannot be exercised by the personal representatives.

3.1 Claim exemptions and reliefs

The task of claiming exemptions and reliefs falls on the personal representatives.

Claiming exemptions and reliefs is the most obvious and straightforward step that can be taken to mitigate the tax due on an inheritance.

Not all exemptions and reliefs are granted automatically, by any means; the personal representatives have to make sure that they *claim* them. They are claimed when details of the estate are submitted to HMRC, using the standard forms supplied by HMRC, together with supporting evidence.

If there is a nil-rate band that can be transferred you should make sure that it is transferred, using the HMRC form (currently IHT 402) within two years of the date of death.

If there is a business amongst the assets of the deceased, you need to look into the availability of BPR (1.17.1); if the estate includes any agricultural property, you need to check for the availability of APR (1.17.4); and if there is any woodland in the estate you should consider taking advantage of woodlands relief (1.17.5). If quick succession relief (QSR) (see 4.8) is available, make sure it is claimed.

Personal representatives can download documents from the HMRC website to claim these reliefs (**www.hmrc.gov.uk**). The main form used for submitting details of an estate to HMRC where there is inheritance tax to pay is known as an IHT 400; the forms used to claim reliefs include:

- 'IHT 413 Business or partnership interests or assets' (i.e., for claiming BPR)
- 'IHT 414 Agricultural Relief'.

There is no special separate form for claiming quick succession relief; it is brought into the IHT calculation in the IHT 400.

Having said that, in many (if not all) cases, it is advisable to instruct a solicitor or accountant to complete the forms.

3.2 Be aware of the tools at your disposal

There are a number of tools available to reduce the burden of inheritance tax on an inheritance that you receive when someone dies, but in practice these will only work to reduce IHT if there are particular circumstances that you can take advantage of.

The tools enable the beneficiaries (that is, the persons who will receive the inheritance) under a will (or beneficiaries of an estate inherited under the intestacy rules) to rewrite the provisions of the will; or even to rewrite the provisions of intestacy for their particular estate.

There are essentially three tools in the toolbox:

1. deeds of variation
2. disclaimers
3. transfers out of trusts.

Collectively, these tools could be referred to as 'post-death rearrangements', as they alter the disposition of an estate after the death has occurred.

3.3 Deeds of variation*

A beneficiary can rewrite the provisions of a will (insofar as those provisions apply to him or her) by means of a document known as a 'deed of variation' (sometimes referred to as a 'deed of family arrangement').

If there are several beneficiaries and they want to rewrite more or less the entire will, they all have to be party to the deed of variation.

If there is a trust in the will, it may prove impossible to rewrite the will, or at least the section of the will containing the trust, using a deed of variation – but other options may be available.

Example 1

Sam has died, having made a will which leaves his entire estate to his son Jed. Jed is independently wealthy and wants to pass the estate to his brother Pete. He can sign a deed of variation which will act to pass Sam's estate to Pete. In order for the variation created by the deed to be treated as a provision made by Sam's will, rather than merely a gift from Jed to Pete, the deed of variation will have to be signed within two years of Sam's death. Deeds of variation are normally prepared by solicitors who specialise in probate matters.

I must emphasise that if the deed of variation is properly made and signed within the two-year time limit, the transfer of Sam's estate from Jed to Pete will not be a PET made by Jed; for inheritance tax purposes, it will be treated as if Sam's will had given Sam's estate to Pete.

*A DOV may be useful where a spouse/CP has the benefit of a transferable NRB from a prior marriage or civil partnership. If no arrangements have been put in place to make use of this, his executors could claim the transferable nil-rate band from his first marriage and a DOV could redirect a share of his estate to a discretionary trust, maximising the IHT savings from his NRBs. (As in 1.12.3). In some cases, it may be possible to implement this arrangement after the death of the second spouse or CP, if the deaths occur within two years of one another.

Example 2

Kulvinder has died, leaving his estate to his adult children, one of whom is his son Bada. Bada can sign a deed of variation which will redirect *his own share* of his father's estate to someone else; he cannot sign a deed of variation which will redirect the entire estate to someone else.

If the entire estate is to be redirected (e.g. to their uncle), all the children will have to sign a deed of variation. This could be in the form of a single document or they could each sign a separate document.

Example 3

Bert has made a will which gives his entire estate to a discretionary trust. (You may recall from 1.24 that a discretionary trust is a trust which does not specify the benefits that any of the beneficiaries will receive from the trust fund; the decisions about the benefits that will be conferred on them are left for the trustees to decide. In other words, benefits are given at the discretion of the trustees – hence the name 'discretionary trust'). The beneficiaries of the trust are his four adult children, their descendants and certain charities.

None of the beneficiaries could individually sign a deed of variation which would redirect his or her share of the estate. This is because none of them is entitled to a share of the estate – but, rather, to a share of the trust established by the estate; and it is up to the trustees of the trust to decide who will receive anything from the trust.

However, if the trustees make arrangements to transfer money, property or other assets out of a discretionary will trust to a beneficiary more than three months from the date of death, but less than two years from the date of death, the transfer will be treated as if it had been a provision in the will. This can bring about the same effect as could be obtained by using a deed of variation, in a situation where a deed of variation would not be available.

So if the trustees appoint £20,000 to Alan, a beneficiary of the trust, eight months after Bert's death, this will be treated for IHT purposes as if Bert's will had contained a gift of £20,000 to Alan.

Planning issues

- The distribution of the estate can be varied whether or not there is a will.
- Property which has passed by operation of the law rather than by a will or the rules of intestacy can be redirected (e.g. a share in a joint bank account which has passed by survivorship to the other joint owner).
- A gift or share of an estate to a beneficiary who has died can be varied subject to the variation taking place within the usual time limits.
- The variation must be used to redirect money, property and assets and cannot be used simply to give executors and trustees further powers. (Further powers can be added to personal representatives if they form part of a redirection of property, e.g. the formation of a trust with assets redirected into it.)
- The parties to a deed must consent to the variation and must be adult. It follows that a minor's share of the estate cannot normally be varied. However, it may be possible to obtain a court order on occasion to vary a minor's share.
- There can be more than one variation from an estate, but property cannot be redirected after having already been redirected.
- The variation must be in writing if the tax benefits are to apply.
- The deed of variation must be signed by the person or persons who would have benefited from the provisions which have been varied, had they not been varied.
- The variation must take place within two years of the date of death.

- The deed of variation must refer to the provisions of the will or the dispositions of the estate under the rules of intestacy which are to be varied. That is to say, the deed must state something along the lines of "The will of X is to be varied"; or "The distribution of the estate of X under the rules of intestacy is to be varied". And it must spell out clearly what provision is to be changed and how it is to be changed, so as to leave no room for doubt.
- The deed must contain a statement by the persons making the variation that the relevant tax laws are to apply.
- The variation must not be for money or any other form of consideration, i.e. it must be gratuitous. Particular care must be taken on this point. Even the issue of who pays for the preparation of the deed can have adverse implications.
- The Conservative government wanted to remove deeds of variation in 1989, but subsequently withdrew the clauses in the finance bill that would have repealed the ability to vary an estate with tax benefits. Five years later the Labour party stated that it would repeal deeds of variation when elected (however, it did not do so). It follows that deeds of variation may not remain as part of the tax planning landscape for the indefinite future, and your planning should not rely on DOVs (deeds of variation) remaining available indefinitely.
- Any deed of variation should be prepared by a qualified legal advisor. This is a generic piece of advice which applies to all the documents referred to in this and the other sections of this book.

3.4 Disclaimers*

A disclaimer is simply a refusal by a beneficiary to accept a gift from an estate or a share of the estate.

The refusal to accept the gift or share means that the gift returns to the estate and is redirected as per the provisions of the will (if there is one) or the rules of intestacy (if there is not).

The beneficiary who disclaims cannot redirect the gift or share that he or she has disclaimed. Disclaiming is therefore less flexible as a tax-planning instrument than deeds of variation and seldom as attractive.

A disclaimer may be appropriate in circumstances where a deed of variation cannot be used. Such circumstances may arise when a beneficiary receives a benefit from a trust in which the deceased was a beneficiary, rather than from the estate of the deceased. In this particular set of circumstances, a deed of variation cannot be used to redirect the interest from the trust that the beneficiary will receive, but a disclaimer may do the job.

Planning issues

- A beneficiary can only make a disclaimer if he has received no benefit from the gift or share of the estate that he wishes to disclaim. He will generally be treated as having accepted the gift, even if all he has received is income from the gift or share rather than the gift or share itself.
- If a disclaimer is to be effective for IHT purposes it must be in writing and made within two years of the date of death.
- The disclaimer must not be made for money or any other form of consideration (as above, with deeds of variation).

*The consequences of a disclaimer are not always straightforward – so do take advice before proceeding down this route!

3.5 Transfers out of trusts

If the deceased has set up a discretionary trust (1.24.2) in his will, this can be used to vary the dispositions of the will without recourse to either a deed of variation or a disclaimer. If there is a transfer of money, property or assets out of the trust to a beneficiary more than three months from the date of death, and less than two years from the date of death, the transfer from the trust is treated as a disposition contained in the will (see 3.3, Example 3, above).

Planning issues

- The appointment must be made by the trustees of the trust rather than the beneficiaries.
- There will be no exit charge on property leaving the trust.
- The appointment is treated for tax purposes as if it had been contained in the will.

3.6 Using the tools

There are a limited number of opportunities to use these tools to mitigate IHT if you are the beneficiary of an estate. The following suggestions will assist you to make the most of the opportunities that present themselves.

3.7 Redirecting to spouse/civil partner

It occasionally happens that an individual who is married or in a civil partnership will leave part of his estate to the surviving spouse or CP, and part of his estate to his children. The result can be an immediate charge to inheritance tax if the share of the estate left to the children exceeds the individual's nil-rate band. This charge to inheritance tax could be eliminated by the judicious use of a deed of variation.

Example

Joe dies, leaving an estate valued at £2.5 million.

He gives £1,250,000 of this to his wife Mary, and the remaining £1,250,000 to his daughter Kate.

The £1,250,000 given to Mary is tax-free, as Mary has the benefit of the spouse exemption.

The £1,250,000 given to Kate will be subject to inheritance tax. Taking into account Joe's nil-rate band, the tax payable on Kate's inheritance will be £370,000:

	£
Value of Kate's legacy:	1,250,000
Less: NRB	(325,000)
	925,000
	£225,000 @ 40% 370,000

Kate could make a deed of variation giving her share of the estate to her mother Mary. If Kate were to make a deed of variation giving her £1,250,000 to Mary, it would be deemed to pass to Mary under the provisions of Joe's will, and would be tax-free due to the spouse exemption.

At a future date, Mary could give the money back to Kate in the form of a PET. Provided that Mary survived the PET by a period of seven years, Kate would have received her inheritance tax-free.

Warning

As previously noted, a deed of variation will not be effective for IHT purposes if it is made for money or for money's worth or for any form of similar personal benefit. Therefore a deed of variation will not be effective in mitigating IHT if it is made to direct money, property or assets to one person with the intention that the person who receives the money etc will just give it back.

The scheme outlined above would be planned in advance by the parties (Kate and Mary), and, as such, would (on the face of it) fail because Mary would intend to give the money back to Kate, after Kate had directed it to Mary via a deed of variation.

However, there are evidential issues which might enable Mary and Kate to carry out the scheme successfully. How would HMRC know what Mary's intention was when Kate signed the deed of variation? There would be no hard evidence as to Mary's intentions at that time.

Mary's intentions may be apparent if Kate signs the deed of variation on Monday, gives Mary the money on Tuesday, and Mary hands it back on Wednesday. But what if there is a significant lapse of time between the deed of variation directing money to Mary and the PET directing money back to Kate? What if the sums of money involved are different?

In such circumstances Mary's intentions may be impossible to prove, even on the balance of probabilities. Kate may well receive her inheritance tax-free.

This book cannot advocate tax evasion

Since this scheme may be tantamount to tax evasion, this book cannot possibly suggest that you consider it. Suffice it to say that hypothetically it would appear to have good prospects of success if implemented carefully.

HMRC are aware that DOVs (deeds of variation) may be open to abuse in this way and have issued some interesting guidance to tax inspectors in their IHT manual. This guidance is quoted in Appendix 2.

Hypothetical planning issues

- HMRC will almost certainly raise awkward questions about the transaction as soon as it becomes aware that there has been a deed of variation in favour of the surviving spouse (or civil partner). How your legal advisor responds to these questions will be one of the factors that are critical to the success of the scheme.
- It may help if the parties (Kate and Mary in the example) are independently advised.
- Your legal advisor may want to obtain counsel's opinion before proceeding.
- Given the risks and the possible need for counsel's opinion, implementing such a scheme will not be cheap and will probably only be worthwhile if there is a significant amount of tax at stake.
- A suitable period between the deed of variation and the PET may be from at least three months to as long as two years.
- If there is a large amount of tax at stake, it will be worth the wait.
- There are risks – e.g. the recipient could become mentally incapable and unable to make a PET before a reasonably safe waiting period has expired.
- If the PET is successful (i.e. if the donor survives for seven years) there will be no requirement to inform HMRC about it and HMRC may be none the wiser.
- If the PET fails (i.e. the person who passes the money back dies within seven years) the tax position should not have been adversely affected, because the deed of variation should have restored the transferable NRB of the first spouse to die. However, the PET will need to be reported as chargeable and may give rise to further

awkward questions. Hypothetically speaking, you and your advisors might have to be prepared to answer some difficult questions very carefully if this were to be the case.

- Not for the faint hearted. By far and away the best thing would be to anticipate the problem in advance of the will and death. It would have been a trifling matter, and perfectly legal, to have left the entire £2.5million to the wife, who could then have given half as a PET to the daughter under her own steam; or to have limited the gift to the daughter to the value of the nil-rate band.

3.8 Maximising BPR and/or APR (double-dip)

Business property relief (BPR) and agricultural property relief (APR) can be maximised by taking advantage of a double-dip will scheme. (See 2.17.) If the deceased did not make a will incorporating this scheme, it could be introduced using a deed of variation.

3.9 Transferring growth tax-free

Individual assets or even an entire estate can sometimes rapidly and substantially increase in value. This may seem unlikely in times such as the credit crunch of 2008-2009, or when an economy is emerging all too slowly from a recession. However, it frequently can happen, and certainly has occurred often in past housing booms.

When this happens, it can present an opportunity to pass on the benefits of growth tax-free.

Example

Kulvinder died in 2010, leaving his entire estate worth £1,000,000 to his wife Suzanne. His estate included shares in a mining company called You've Never Had It So Good Plc, valued at £300,000. A year and a half after the date of his death, the company discovered new valuable mineral reserves in land it held which had previously been considered almost worthless, and the shares almost tripled in value to £800,000.

Suzanne could make a deed of variation, giving the shares in You've Never Had It So Good Plc to her and Kulvinder's daughter Avril. For IHT purposes, Avril would be deemed to have received the shares at the value they had at the date of death of her father, i.e. £300,000, so there would be no IHT to pay, as this would be covered by her late father's nil-rate band.

Avril would therefore have received assets valued at £800,000 tax-free from her late father's estate.

This transaction would use up the majority of Kulvinder's nil-rate band, so there would not be a great deal left to transfer to Suzanne's estate on her death to mitigate IHT payable on Suzanne's estate. However, the transferable nil-rate band would be unlikely to reach the dizzy heights of £800,000 for a long time, so it seems the best choice. The NRB, at the time of writing in 2010, was currently frozen (possibly for a number of years) at £325,000 and in any event rises (or is intended to rise) only in line with inflation.

Given that inflation is currently low, a leap to £800,000 is not going to happen any time soon. The only way it might occur is if the Conservative party were to carry out its declared ambition of raising the NRB to £1,000,000. Even if it did this (which is currently unfeasible in the context of a coalition government) it is not clear whether it would permit the increased NRB to be transferable. In fact, there is no guarantee that the transferable NRB will survive future governments and it remains to be seen how long it will last.

If the rise in value of the shares in You've Never Had It So Good Plc seems implausible, take a moment to consider the housing booms and the bull markets in shares we have seen since (say) 1980.

3.10 By-passing a generation

If you are independently wealthy and you have no need of an inheritance, receiving a large sum of money might be of little benefit to you and may only serve to increase the liability of your own estate to inheritance tax at a future date.

If you dispose of the inheritance by making a PET you will have to survive it by a period of seven years in order to be sure that the tax liability for the PET has fallen out of your estate.

If, however, you make a deed of variation diverting the inheritance away from you (say to your children), there will be no seven-year wait, as the gift under the deed of variation will be treated as a gift from the estate of the deceased.

3.11 Giving to charities/political parties etc

If you are in the habit of giving to charities etc, and you receive an inheritance that is subject to inheritance tax, you may feel that it is an appropriate time to make a charitable donation. If you do so using a deed of variation, the charity will receive the gift that you make free of IHT. Any IHT that has been paid can be reclaimed from HMRC by the personal representatives and passed on to the charity.

If, however, you receive a sum of money from the estate and hand it over to the charity without making a deed of variation, some of your largesse will have been bestowed on HMRC.

Note that Gift Aid is a different animal entirely to the charitable exemption granted in respect of inheritance tax. Gift Aid arises via the income and capital gains tax system, and is available in respect of gifts of money made by individuals who pay UK income tax and/or capital gains tax.

Part 4
Dealing With Inheritance Tax Issues on Death if You Are Administering an Estate

4.1 Brief summary of administering an estate (probate)

Administering an estate is the process that has to be taken to deal with the financial affairs of a deceased person. Inheritance tax is an important issue when administering a high value estate, because of the deemed transfer that takes place on death. (See 1.2 and the footnote to 1.2.)

Even if there is no inheritance tax to pay, it is often necessary to complete an inheritance tax account.

The following steps are required to administer an estate:

- register the death
- arrange the funeral
- pay the funeral bill
- make enquiries about the income of the deceased
- value the money, property, assets and debts of the deceased*
- make enquiries into the gifts history of the deceased*

- make enquiries as to whether the deceased has an interest in possession trust (IIP)*
- consider any issues that arise regarding domicile*
- prepare the appropriate IHT account and deliver it to HMRC
- prepare other papers required for probate
- pay inheritance tax if applicable
- apply for probate**
- obtain probate and cash the assets/obtain the money (i.e. send withdrawal forms to the banks, sell or transfer the house, etc)
- pay the debts of the deceased – e.g. credit card bills, outstanding income tax, etc
- pay any administration expenses (i.e. fees of professionals who have provided their services)
- prepare estate accounts
- distribute what is left to the person or persons entitled under the will (or under the rules of intestacy if there is no will).

This is not necessarily an exhaustive list, but serves to indicate the broad sweep of what is required.

---

*These actions are required to determine the liability of the estate (if any) to inheritance tax, and to determine which type of inheritance tax account is required.

**The word 'probate' is often used rather loosely to refer to the process of dealing with the financial affairs of someone who has died. Strictly speaking, probate is a document which you will need to access the money, property, bank accounts and other assets held in the name of a deceased person who has left a will. The full name for this document is a grant of probate. If the deceased person did not make a will, the document that you will need is called a grant of letters of administration. There are many different types of grant, but the grant of probate and grant of letters of administration are the most commonly used types, and the only types that most people require.

4.2 Important time limits and penalties for delay

Missing a time limit can have severe repercussions so it is important to take these into account from an early stage.

Six months

Six months after the date of death, interest begins to be charged on any inheritance tax owed by the estate.

12 months

The IHT account must be filed with HMRC within 12 months of the month in which the death occurred. This is the due date for delivery of the account.

There is a modest amount of lee-way granted to this deadline. The due date for delivery may be extended to a later date than 12 months from the month in which the death occurred, *provided that the account is delivered within three months of the date the personal representatives began acting as PRs.*

If the PRs fail to comply with this deadline, there is an initial penalty of £100*.

18 months

If the IHT account is filed with HMRC between six months and 12 months after the due date for delivery, there is a further penalty of £100*.

*Where the due date for delivery of the account expires after 22 January 2005. Different penalties apply if the due date was prior to this.

Two years

Two years is a critical deadline with many possible repercussions should it be missed.

IHT accounts

If you have not filed an IHT account within two years of the date of death and there would have been a liability to tax shown in the account, there is a further penalty of up to £3,000.*

Deeds of variation

There is an absolute deadline of two years from the date of death in which to make a deed of variation that will be treated as a disposition made by the will.

Transfers from trusts

A transfer from a trust set up by the will of the deceased must take place within two years of the date of death (but more than three months from the date of death) in order to be treated as a disposition made by the will. If this time limit is not observed, the transfer will be treated as a transfer from the trust made by the trustees and will be subject to the tax rules that apply in those circumstances (1.24).

Transferable nil-rate band

Claims to transfer the nil-rate band from a predeceased spouse or civil partner must be made within 24 months from the end of the month in which the surviving spouse or civil partner dies (i.e. the spouse or civil partner to whose estate the nil-rate band of the first to die is to be transferred).

---

*This applies where the due date for delivery expires after 22 July 2004. Different penalties apply if the due date was prior to this.

As with IHT accounts, there is a modest amount of lee-way granted to this deadline. The due date for delivery may be extended to a later date than 12 months from the month in which the death occurred, *provided that the account is delivered within three months of the date the personal representatives began acting as PRs.*

Woodlands relief

PRs must make an election for woodlands relief within two years of the date of death.

4.3 Valuations

4.3.1 Death estates – general principles

As noted in 4.1, it is necessary to value the assets held by the deceased. This is obviously an essential requirement to assist with determining the liability of the estate (if any) to IHT.

There are two issues facing PRs with this requirement.

1. The PRs are under an obligation to make the fullest possible enquiries regarding the extent of the money, property and assets held by the deceased.

   If they fail to declare an asset in an account which they submit to HMRC, they could face penalties unless they can demonstrate that they made the fullest possible enquiries and the asset nevertheless did not come to light until after the account had been submitted.

   This means, for instance, that they should not rely on the papers of the deceased to provide the material for the IHT account. If there are shares, the PRs will need to confirm the number of shares held by contacting the share registrars and so on.

2. The PRs must provide accurate values of the assets which reflect the market value* at the date of death. Estimated values may be acceptable if, and only if, the PRs have made the fullest possible enquiries to establish the value of an asset – enquiries that are reasonably practicable in the circumstances – and have nevertheless been unable to establish the exact value of the asset. If an IHT account includes an estimate, it must contain a statement declaring that an estimated value has been used. Estimated values may be subject to investigation by HMRC and if you have used an estimate and prove unable to justify the value claimed in your estimate, you may be lining yourself up for a substantial fine.

4.3.2 Transferors and trustees

Transferors and trustees face similar issues with regard to valuations, as do personal representatives.

On those occasions that they are liable to submit an IHT account, they must provide accurate values of the property transferred. The use of an incorrect value – whether fraudulent, intentional, reckless or negligent – will incur a fine. (Possibly a substantial one.)

4.3.3 Market value

The market value is generally the amount that would be paid on the open market by a willing buyer to a willing seller negotiating at arm's length.

There are exceptions to this general rule.

* "Except as otherwise provided by this Act, the value at any time of any property shall for the purposes of this Act be the price which the property might reasonably be expected to fetch if sold in the open market at that time; but that price shall not be assumed to be reduced on the ground that the whole property is to be placed on the market at one and the same time." (IHTA 1984 s160)

- Changes in the value resulting from the death itself may be taken into account. E.g. valuations of the personal goodwill element of a business may be reduced to take into account the loss of the business owner.*
- Related property is taken into account.**
- Restrictions on the freedom to dispose of a property are generally ignored unless the freedom has been curtailed in exchange for money or for money's worth.

---

*"(1) In determining the value of a person's estate immediately before his death, changes in the value of his estate, which have occurred by reason of the death and fall within subsection (2) below, shall be taken into account as if they had occurred before the death.

"(2) A change falls within this subsection if it is an addition to the property comprised in the estate or an increase or decrease of the value of any property so comprised, other than a decrease resulting from such an alteration as is mentioned in section 98(1) above; but the termination on the death of any interest or the passing of any interest by survivorship does not fall within this subsection." (IHTA 1984 s171)

**"Where the value of any property comprised in a person's estate would be less than the appropriate portion of the value of the aggregate of that and any related property, it shall be the appropriate portion of the value of that aggregate.

"(2) For the purposes of this section, property is related to the property comprised in a person's estate if —

"(a) it is comprised in the estate of his spouse [F1or civil partner] ; or

"(b) it is or has within the preceding five years been —

"(i) the property of a charity, or held on trust for charitable purposes only, or

"(ii) the property of a body mentioned in section 24, [F224A,][F3or 25] above,

"and became so on a transfer of value which was made by him or his spouse F1or civil partner after 15th April 1976 and was exempt to the extent that the value transferred was attributable to the property...." (IHTA 1984 s161)

4.3.4 Valuations of specific types of property

Land

If land is co-owned, the co-owners may be able to claim a reduced value of their respective shares for IHT purposes to reflect the fact that the sale of a half share in (say) a house might be problematical. (The purchaser might have to be willing to occupy the house with a co-owner he did not know.) The discount available is usually 10%-15%.

The discount is applicable to lifetime transfers and to the deemed transfer on death.

The discount is not normally available if the co-owners are spouses or CPs. (Because of the related property rules – see the next section below.)

There is no similar discount where an asset is jointly owned but does not happen to be land. So, for example, there would be no discount on a jointly-held shareholding even if the co-owners were not spouses or CPs.

Related property

The related property rules prevent spouses and CPs from making exempt transfers of valuable property to each other to devalue the property for IHT purposes.

As previously noted, a set or collection of items can be worth more than the sum of the individual items. E.g. a complete set of Chippendale chairs will be worth more than the individual chairs; the shares in a shareholding which is large enough to confer control of a company will be worth more than shares which do not confer such control.

If an individual transfers, for example, some of his controlling shares to his spouse or CP, to the extent that the shares he retains no longer confer control his remaining shares will be much devalued. He could then transfer his remaining shares to a third party, incurring a lesser charge to IHT than would otherwise have been the case.

The related property rules prevent this. They provide for the property that has been transferred to the spouse or CP to be aggregated with any property transferred to a third party (or transferred on death), and for IHT to be imposed accordingly.

Quoted shares

The price of quoted shares is best worked out by referring the matter to a stockbroker! Having said that, the HMRC website* suggests that the closing price of the shares on the day of death can be used, and could be obtained "by looking at the financial pages of a newspaper, or by looking on the newspaper's website or a commercial website". So presumably this approach is acceptable – as long as you don't make a mistake! (See section 4.4 about penalties – below.)

A brief explanation may be required at this point. The closing price refers to the price of the shares in the last trade that takes place at the end of the trading day.

On some occasions, there may be a range of closing prices for the shares. If so, the 'quarter-up' method is used. Your broker should know about this and provide a valuation on the 'quarter-up' basis. HMRC also helpfully explain how to do it. If the range is given as 1091p to 1101p, you would work out the 'quarter up' price following these steps:

> **Step one:** find the difference between the higher price and the lower price: 1101p -1091p = 10p
>
> **Step two:** work out a quarter of the difference between the two prices: 10p / 0.25 = 2.5p

*The page is called 'How to value stocks and shares for inheritance tax' – **www.hmrc.gov.uk/inheritancetax/how-to-value-estate/shares.html**

Step three: add a quarter of the difference to the lower price: 1091p + 2.5p = 1093.5p

So the quarter-up price is 1093.5p and the value of the 1,000 shares is £10,935 (1,000 / 1093.5p).

Easy!

As there are sometimes other factors involved in valuing quoted shares, engaging a professional is the approach that should be taken in the majority of cases.

Unquoted shares

Shares in unquoted companies are difficult to value as there is often no market as such. The approach taken by most (if not all) solicitors is to request an accountant to provide a valuation.

4.4 Penalties for incorrect accounts

From 1 April 2009*, where the due date for filing an IHT account is 1 April 2010, the penalty regime for submitting an incorrect IHT account is as follows.

The approach taken to imposing penalties for incorrect accounts is based on the behaviour of the person responsible for providing the information, the gravity of the offence and the amount of tax at stake. Note that the word 'incorrect' can have a wide meaning and can apply to any inaccuracy that could lead to a lower amount of tax being charged than should be the case.

No penalty will be charged where the person responsible for supplying the information takes "reasonable care"**. Penalties are charged where the individual fails to take reasonable care; or deliberately submits an incorrect document.

If the individual brings the inaccuracy to the attention of HMRC "unprompted"***, the penalty will be lower than if he is "prompted" to do so.

1. If you can demonstrate that you have taken "reasonable care", there is no penalty (other than having to pay the additional tax liability).
2. If you were "careless" and your disclosure of the error was "unprompted*" the minimum penalty is zero and the maximum penalty is 30% of the additional tax liability (along with, obviously, paying the additional tax liability).
3. If you were "careless" and your disclosure of the error was "prompted", the minimum penalty is 15% and the maximum penalty is 30% of the additional tax liability (along with, obviously, paying the additional tax liability).
4. If the error in the account was "deliberate" and your disclosure of the error was "unprompted", the minimum penalty is 20% and the maximum penalty is 70% of the additional tax liability (along with, obviously, paying the additional tax liability).
5. If the error in the account was "deliberate" and your disclosure of the error was "prompted" the minimum penalty is 35% and the maximum penalty is 70% of the additional tax liability (along with, obviously, paying the additional tax liability).

---

*The penalty regime prior to this date was not noticeably more generous to the taxpayer!

**Stories abound of penalties being charged where taxpayers appear to have taken what many people would consider to be "reasonable care". For instance, an executor called Mr Colin Lever submitted an inheritance tax account which included the valuation of a house at £1.4 million. Mr Lever had obtained this valuation from a professional firm. The house sold at auction for £2 million six weeks' later. Mr Lever paid inheritance tax on the full £2 million. Despite this, HMRC suggested that Mr Lever should personally have to pay a penalty of £44,700 for delivering an incorrect inheritance tax account!

The full story and the outcome – the penalty was reduced to nil after a long, hard struggle – can be read in Mr Lever's own words in *Taxation* magazine (**www.taxation.co.uk/taxation/articles/2010/01/20/19849/executor-trial**).

***"Unprompted" means that you disclose an inaccuracy to HMRC at a time that you have no reason to suppose that they might know about it already.

6. If the error in the account was "deliberate and concealed" and your disclosure of the error was "unprompted", the minimum penalty is 30% and the maximum penalty is 100% of the additional tax liability (along with, obviously, paying the additional tax liability).
7. Finally, if the error in the account was "deliberate and concealed" and your disclosure of the error was "prompted", the minimum penalty is 50% and the maximum penalty is 100% of the additional tax liability (along with, obviously, paying the additional tax liability).

4.5 Liability to deliver accounts

Curiously there is sometimes a distinction made between the person who is deemed to be liable to submit an IHT account, and the person who is liable to pay the tax.

4.5.1 Lifetime transfers – PETs

If an individual makes a PET, he has no liability to deliver an IHT account for a PET, and nor has the transferee.

If the individual dies and the PET becomes chargeable, the individual's personal representatives are responsible for submitting details of the PET in an IHT account.

4.5.2 Lifetime chargeable transfers

If an individual makes a lifetime chargeable transfer (1.15), he must submit an account (currently an IHT 100) notifying HMRC of the property to which IHT is attributable, the value of the property and the date of the transfer.

Generally an account must be submitted even if the chargeable transfer is within the nil-rate band of the transferor. However, there is no requirement to submit a return if:

- the transfer is a transfer of cash, quoted shares or securities only, and the value of the gift together with any chargeable transfers made in the previous seven years does not exceed the current inheritance tax nil-rate band
- or the amount of the gift, after exemptions and any other chargeable transfers made in the last seven years, is not more than 80% of the current nil-rate band, and the transfer of value (before exemptions), together with the value of all chargeable transfers made in the last seven years, does not exceed the IHT nil-rate band
- or the chargeable transfer arises from the termination of a life interest and the life tenant has given the trustees notice informing them of the availability of an annual exemption, or marriage and civil partnership gift exemption, and the exemption covers the whole of the value transferred.

If a transferor dies within seven years of making a chargeable transfer, his PRs must include details of the chargeable transfer in their IHT account, even if an IHT 100 has been submitted by the transferor.

4.5.3 Transfers on death

The persons principally responsible for submitting an IHT account on the death of an individual are his or her PRs.

They must submit an account to the HMRC Capital Taxes Office in Nottingham. (HM revenue and Customs, Inheritance Tax, Ferrers House, PO Box 38, Castle Meadow Road, Nottingham NG2 1BB.)

The account is given on an official form, the IHT 400, and usually requires a number of supporting forms with IHT prefixes (e.g. IHT 403 to submit details of lifetime gifts) and evidence (such as a copy of the will if there is one). The account includes details of all the estate of the deceased immediately prior to death and of all chargeable transfers (including failed PETs) made by the deceased within seven years of his or her death (or 14 years in exceptional circumstances – 1.15.6, 1.15.7)*.

A person who has received a PET which has increased their estate will also be liable to submit an account.

The time limits for submission of accounts have been given at 4.2.

Certain consequences arise with regard to the liability to deliver an account if no grant is obtained within 12 months of the end of the month in which the deceased died (4.2).

The liability to deliver an account is imposed on other individuals in addition to the PRs:

> (1) every person in whom any of the property forming part of the estate vests (whether beneficially or otherwise) on or at any time after the deceased's death or who at any such time is beneficially entitled to an interest in possession in any such property, and
>
> (2) where any of the property is at any such time comprised in a settlement and there is no person beneficially entitled to an interest in possession in that property, every person for whose benefit any of that property (or income from it) is applied at any such time, shall deliver to the Board an account specifying to the best of his knowledge and belief the appropriate property vested in him, in which he has an interest or which (or income from which) is applicable for his benefit and the value of that property.**

---

*"...where an account is to be delivered by personal representatives...the appropriate property is—

"(a) all property which formed part of the deceased's estate immediately before his death...and

"(b) all property to which was attributable the value transferred by any chargeable transfers made by the deceased within seven years of his death.." (IHTA s216(3))

**IHTA 1984 s216

The liability to deliver an account applies whether or not there is any inheritance tax payable on the estate.

However, if the estate is what is known as an 'excepted estate', there is no need to deliver a full account.*** Instead, a simplified document known as an IHT 205 (2006) should be completed. This does not need to be submitted to HMRC; it is sent to the Probate Registry when applying for a grant.

It would be helpful to be able to describe in a few words the difference between an excepted estate and one in which there is no tax to pay. Unfortunately, this is not possible. The definition of an excepted estate is extremely complex.**** The following points can be made.

- There are some estates which are taxable. All of these require the submission of a full IHT account (currently known as an IHT 400).
- Some estates are not taxable but still require submission of a full IHT account.
- Some estates are not taxable and are excepted estates. These require only the submission of the simplified Estate Information Form IHT 205.

The easiest way to ascertain whether a full IHT account is required is probably to read through the IHT 205 (2006) and the notes to help you fill in the IHT 205 (2006) – IHT 206 (2006). These can be downloaded from the HMRC website.
(**www.hmrc.gov.uk/agents/forms-iht.htm#1**)

A rough rule of thumb is that:

- if the gross value of an estate is more than £325,000, and there is no spouse or civil partner or charitable exemption available, it will not be an excepted estate

***"No person is required to deliver an account... of the property comprised in an excepted estate." (The Inheritance Tax (Delivery of Accounts) (Excepted Estates) Regulations 2004)

****If you are curious to know more about the complexity, refer to s4 of The Inheritance Tax (Delivery of Accounts) (Excepted Estates) Regulations 2004.

- if the gross value of the estate is more than £1,000,000 it will not be an excepted estate.

4.5.4 Trustees

Trustees must submit IHT accounts in a number of situations.

All trusts

Transfers to trustees, whether lifetime transfers or transfers on death, do not generally require the delivery of an account by the trustees, as the liability to deliver an account is imposed on the transferor. (But note the comments in 4.5.3 about the liability that is imposed when a grant has not been obtained within 12 months of the month in which the death occurred.)

Relevant property trusts

Trustees are required to submit IHT accounts when a liability to tax arises – i.e. when there is a transfer from a trust and on the ten-year anniversary.

Other trusts

Other trusts must submit accounts when chargeable events occur – e.g. on the termination of a qualifying interest in possession and the transfer of value from the trust.

Excepted settlements

Some trusts are excepted from the need to submit IHT returns. The requirements for a trust to be excepted are:

- there is no qualifying interest in possession when a chargeable event occurs
- the chargeable event occurs on or after 6 April 2002
- the only asset in the trust is cash

- the trustees are UK residents and have been throughout the existence of the trust
- the gross value of the trust fund at the time of the chargeable event does not exceed £1,000
- there are no related trusts.

4.6 Loss relief on sale of land

When there is land (or an interest in land) in an estate, the PRs will normally have a professional valuation made and include details on their IHT return.

Sometimes when PRs sell the land after the death, the land is sold for less than the value declared on the IHT account (and agreed with HMRC). In certain circumstances, the value declared on the IHT account can be replaced by the sale price and a refund of IHT can be claimed on the difference between the two values.* (Because IHT will have been calculated on the higher value.)

The circumstances are that:

- the land (or interest in land) must have been in the estate of the deceased immediately before his death
- it must have been sold by the appropriate person (i.e. the person liable to pay IHT on the land) within the period of four years immediately following the date of the death
- when the land or interest in land was sold, it must have been the same in all respects, in the same state and with the same incidents (i.e. subject to the same tenancies) as at the date of death**

*IHTA s191 and 197A

**If these conditions are not met, the sale value is increased to the value that would have prevailed had the conditions been met. This includes the situation where land is worth less because of the expiry of a lease since the date of death. The value is increased and the increase is "equal to the appropriate fraction of the value on death of the interest". (IHTA 1984 s194)

- the appropriate person must make a claim for the relief, stating the capacity in which he made the claim.

The loss relief is not available:

- if the sale value of the land would differ from its value on death by less than the lower of (a) £1,000, and (b) 5% of its value on death
- or if the sale is a sale by a personal representative or trustee to:
  (i) a person who, at any time between the death and the sale, has been beneficially entitled to, or to an interest in possession in, property comprised in the interest sold, or
  (ii) the spouse or civil partner or a child or remoter descendant of the spouse or civil partner of a person defined in (i); or
  (iii) trustees of a settlement under which a person within sub-paragraph (i) or (ii) above has an interest in possession in property comprising the interest sold
- or if it is a sale in which the vendor or any person within sub-paragraph (i), (ii) or (iii) above obtains a right to acquire the interest sold or any other interest in the same land.

Loss of relief on the sale of land is claimed using form IHT 38.

4.7 Loss of value relief on sale of shares

Loss relief on shares can be claimed where losses are incurred on the sale, cancellation or suspension of qualifying investments within 12 months of the date of death of the deceased*. This is similar to loss relief on the sale of land, but more time limited.

*IHTA 1984 s179

In other words, shares owned by the deceased will have been given a value at the date of death. The date-of-death value will have given rise to a charge to tax. If the shares are subsequently sold for a lower price than the value on which they were taxed at the date of death, the sale price can be substituted for the date of death value, bringing about a refund of tax paid. If the shares are cancelled or suspended, the new value (presumably nil) can be substituted for the value at the date of death.

The qualifying investments for which this privileged treatment is given are shares or securities quoted (i.e. on a recognised stock exchange) at the date of death; unit trusts which are authorised at the date of death; and shares in OEIC's (open-ended investment companies) and any common investment fund.

The relief reduces the value claimed at the date of death of all qualifying investments which have been sold or suspended within the 12 months following the date of death. The relief cannot be 'cherry picked' and applied to only those investments which have made losses when some have not done so. What this means in practice is that if some shares have risen in value and been sold, and some have fallen in value and been sold, then the prices of all the shares that have been sold since the date of death must be substituted for their death values. In the case of the shares that have risen in value, this substitution will create an additional liability to inheritance tax, rather than a reduction. So the relief is only worth claiming where the value of all the shares taken together which have been sold or suspended amounts to less than the date-of-death value.

Loss of value relief on the sale of shares is claimed using form IHT 35.

4.8 Quick succession relief

Quick succession relief provides a measure of relief from IHT charges when there is a transfer on death by an individual within five years of his estate having been increased by a chargeable transfer.

In other words, if an individual has received an inheritance which was subject to inheritance tax, and died within five years of receiving it, there may be some possibility of receiving a refund of the tax paid on the inheritance of that he received prior to his death.

The amount of relief given is between 20% and 100% and depends on the time from the first transfer to the death. It is applied to the first transfer and is therefore of no help if no tax was paid on the first transfer.

4.9 Liability to pay the tax

4.9.1 Person on whom liability is imposed

The liability to pay IHT may be imposed (by the action of the Inheritance Tax Act 1984 s199 and s200) on any of the following:

- the transferor
- the transferee
- the PRs of the deceased
- the beneficiaries.

If a transferor makes a chargeable transfer during his lifetime, he is principally liable to pay the tax (see 1.15).

If the transferor does not pay it, the transferee becomes liable to pay the tax.

If the tax remains uncollected at the date of death of the transferor, the transferee remains liable.

If a PET becomes chargeable because the transferor dies within seven years of making it, the transferee is liable to pay the tax.*

In practice, the personal representatives will submit an IHT 400 which will include details of lifetime gifts on supplementary page 403. HMRC will use this information to attempt to obtain payment of the IHT liability from the transferee. If this is not possible (e.g. because the transferee cannot be traced or has left the country) HMRC will approach the personal representatives for payment of the liability.

4.9.2 The death estate – burden of inheritance tax on gifts in wills

If the deceased has left a professionally drawn-up will, the will should specify what part of his estate will bear the tax payable. A will normally makes gifts "free of tax" or (rarely) "subject to tax".

If a will makes a gift free of tax (e.g. "I give the sum of £10,000 free of tax, to Diane", the tax on the gift is paid by the PRs from the residue; see 1.22).

If a will makes a gift subject to tax, the tax is borne by the recipient of the gift.

If the will is silent as to who bears the tax on a gift, determining the tax consequences can be difficult, and for complex situations it will be beyond the scope of this book. In the majority of situations, wills make straightforward gifts of money. E.g. "I give £10,000 to Diane". If a will is silent about the burden of tax on such a gift, the tax is borne by the residue. If the gift is a gift of land, e.g. "I give my dwelling house to Alan" and the will is silent as to the burden of tax, the tax will be borne by the recipient of the gift.

---

*The persons liable for the tax on the value transferred by a chargeable transfer made (under section 4 above) on the death of any person are "so far as the tax is attributable to the value of any property, any person in whom the property is vested (whether beneficially or otherwise) at any time after the death..." (IHTA 1984 s200)

If a will makes a gift free of tax, the residue will bear the tax payable on it. If the residue (or a share of the residue) is given to an exempt beneficiary (such as a spouse or a charity), this will lead to the unfortunate phenomenon of "grossing up", discussed in 1.15 in connection with chargeable transfers.

Grossing up is based on the principle that to arrive at any given sum tax-free, you must start out with a higher sum. E.g. assume that a will makes a tax-free gift of £90,000.

In order to give the sum of £300,000 tax-free, the personal representatives must start with a gift of £500,000, which, subject to tax at the death rate of 40%, will achieve a taxed figure of £300,000, since 40% of £500,000 is £200,000 (and £500,000 - £200,000 = £300,000).

Turning this calculation around, to arrive at the tax-free figure for any chargeable gift on death, you must start with the tax-free figure that you want, then gross it up by 5/3. You will note in the foregoing example that £500,000 is 5/3 of £300,000.

Grossing up on the death estate has more severe consequences than grossing up on chargeable transfers. With chargeable transfers, the transfer is grossed up by multiplying it by 5/4 before the tax is charged at 20%; on a transfer on death, the factor is 5/3 as the tax is charged at 40%.

Note that liability for payment of tax on lifetime gifts remains principally with the recipients of such gifts (4.9.1).

Example

A house valued at £180,000 has been given to Frances, free of tax. The residue is given to a charity.

The tax is calculated as follows:

	£
Chargeable amount:	180,000
Multiplied by the gross up factor of 5/3:	300,000
£300,000 taxed at death rate of 40%:	**£120,000**

(Note that £300,000 less the tax due of £120,000 gives the original value of the gifted house: £180,000.)

The estate must part with a total of £300,000 in order to release a gift worth £180,000!

4.9.3 Burden of inheritance tax if there is no will (intestacy)

If there is no will, any IHT payable on the death estate is paid by the PRs of the deceased from the residuary estate.

There will be no tax-free gifts, other than for the share of the estate given to the surviving spouse.

Note that liability for payment of tax on lifetime gifts remains principally with the recipients of such gifts (4.9.1).

4.10 Dealing with the IHT 205 (2006) and IHT 400

If an estate is an excepted estate, an IHT 205 (2006) should be completed and submitted to the Probate Registry. The IHT 205 can be downloaded from the HMRC website (**www.hmrc.gov.uk/agents/forms-iht.htm#1**).

If you are administering an estate which you believe to be an excepted estate and you are correct in your belief, there is a case to be made that you could complete the document yourself and avoid professional fees. However, it is probably only safe to do so only in those cases where there is definitely no prospect that you could be mistaken about the estate being excepted.

If it should prove otherwise, you could be subject to a penalty for an incorrect return (see above; 4.4).

If an estate requires an IHT 400 and no IHT is payable, the same case could be made – that you could complete the document yourself and avoid professional fees. Bear in mind that, if you are wrong about the IHT situation, the saving on professional fees could be illusory after the (almost inevitable) penalty.

If an IHT 400 is required because IHT is payable, it probably makes more sense to pay professional fees than to risk the consequences of not paying them.

Conclusion

Inheritance tax planning is to be recommended if your estate may be subject to a level of taxation that you regard as excessive. As we've seen, it could save your heirs a great deal of money and stress.

However, please bear in mind that any tax planning you take could impact adversely on your own lifestyle. Given the varying circumstances of every reader, this is obviously something that no book can hope to truly explore – a whole range of unique factors will come into play, depending on income, savings, pension plans and other assets, as well as living arrangements. The details of the inheritance tax regime, and what steps can be taken to minimise its burden, are all that a guide like this can go into, and I have only sought to raise the issue of affecting your present way of life in the text where it seemed specially pertinent. It is, nonetheless, the essential balance to be struck when making any arrangements regarding inheritance tax.

When you take measures to reduce the tax burden on your estate it is essential that you retain sufficient wealth to meet your own needs for the foreseeable future. Likewise, do not fall for the attractive trap of dramatically rearranging your life simply in order to protect assets from the taxman. As we have seen, there are enough simple steps that can be taken, with prudent timing, to mean that more acrobatic or extreme measures are rarely necessary, and even more rarely advisable.

Appendices

Appendix 1: Historical rates of nil-rate bands

The information below is helpfully published by HMRC on their website **www.hmrc.gov.uk**, along with other useful information.

Inheritance tax thresholds – present day back to 18 March 1986		
From	**To**	**Threshold/nil-rate band**
6 April 2009	–	£325,000
6 April 2008	5 April 2009	£312,000
6 April 2007	5 April 2008	£300,000
6 April 2006	5 April 2007	£285,000
6 April 2005	5 April 2006	£275,000
6 April 2004	5 April 2005	£263,000
6 April 2003	5 April 2004	£255,000
6 April 2002	5 April 2003	£250,000
6 April 2001	5 April 2002	£242,000
6 April 2000	5 April 2001	£234,000
6 April 1999	5 April 2000	£231,000
6 April 1998	5 April 1999	£223,000
6 April 1997	5 April 1998	£215,000
6 April 1996	5 April 1997	£200,000
6 April 1995	5 April 1996	£154,000
10 March 1992	5 April 1995	£150,000
6 April 1991	9 March 1992	£140,000
6 April 1990	5 April 1991	£128,000
6 April 1989	5 April 1990	£118,000
15 March 1988	5 April 1989	£110,000
17 March 1987	14 March 1988	£90,000
18 March 1986	16 March 1987	£71,000

'Capital transfer tax' (inheritance tax thresholds) – 17 March 1986 back to 13 March 1975		
England, Wales, Scotland and Northern Ireland		
6 April 1985	17 March 1986	£67,000
13 March 1984	5 April 1985	£64,000
15 March 1983	12 March 1984	£60,000
9 March 1982	14 March 1983	£55,000
26 March 1980	8 March 1982	£50,000
27 October 1977	25 March 1980	£25,000
13 March 1975	26 October 1977	£15,000

'Estate Duty' (inheritance tax thresholds) – 12 March 1975 back to 16 August 1914		
England, Wales and Scotland		
22 March 1972	12 March 1975	£15,000
31 March 1971	21 March 1972	£12,500
16 April 1969	30 March 1971	£10,000
4 April 1963	15 April 1969	£5,000
9 April 1962	3 April 1963	£4,000
30 July 1954	8 April 1962	£3,000
10 April 1946	29 July 1954	£2,000
16 August 1914	9 April 1946	£100

Appendix 2: HMRC's view on redirection as avoidance

The following is an excerpt from the HMRC *Inheritance Tax Manual*, which details the HMRC view of schemes along the lines of the theoretical proposal outlined in 3.7.

Before you read the excerpt, an explanation is probably required. What the first paragraph is driving at is the situation where a will gives part of the estate to the surviving spouse or civil partner of the deceased, and part of the estate to (say) the deceased's son, creating a liability to inheritance tax with regard to the son's share, which exceeds the nil-rate band. The son then creates a deed of variation (3.3), which redirects his share of the estate to the surviving spouse, eliminating the charge to inheritance tax as the spouse is exempt from paying inheritance tax due to the spouse exemption (1.8).

This is a pre-planned arrangement, made with the intention that the spouse will give the estate back to the son in the form of a PET; and provided that the spouse survives for the period of seven years after making the PET, the son will not have to pay IHT on the estate received under the will. The charge to IHT will have been eliminated.

A deed of variation made as part of this kind of arrangement will not be a genuine, or 'bona fide', deed of variation, because it will have been made with the intention that the estate that is re-directed by the variation will be directed back to the original beneficiary (the son).

IHTM35093 – Property redirected to the spouse or civil partner: gifts back to original beneficiaries

"This is one of a couple of schemes (see also IHTM35094) where the taxpayer seeks to take advantage of the provisions of IHTA84/S42 without there being a bona fide variation [i.e. a genuine variation]. Most commonly, chargeable beneficiaries will give up benefits under the will in favour of the surviving spouse or civil partner (IHTM11032), thus gaining the benefit of spouse or civil partner exemption, and the spouse or civil partner then returns the benefits to the original beneficiaries. Where a chargeable beneficiary makes an IoV [IoV stands for an 'instrument of variation', which is another way of saying a deed of variation – see 3.3] in favour of the deceased's spouse or civil partner you should ask the taxpayers:

- whether there had been any discussion between the parties before the IoV was made about how the benefit redirected to the spouse or civil partner should be dealt with, and
- whether subsequent to the IoV the spouse or civil partner has made any transfers to the original chargeable beneficiaries, or is contemplating making any such transfers.

The IoV may create an interest in possession (IHTM16061) trust for the surviving spouse or civil partner, but the trustees have a power of appointment by which they can appoint capital to other beneficiaries including, usually, the original beneficiaries under the will. Where this applies, the second question above should be amended to ask whether the trustees have already exercised the power of appointment or whether an exercise of it is contemplated.

(This text has been withheld because of exemptions in the Freedom of Information Act 2000) [These omission notices appear in the original.]

(This text has been withheld because of exemptions in the Freedom of Information Act 2000)

(This text has been withheld because of exemptions in the Freedom of Information Act 2000)

Where the answers to those questions indicate any possibility that the spouse or civil partner may not retain all the redirected benefits, you should refer the case immediately to TG.*"

*This rather implies that where the answers do not indicate any possibility that the spouse or CP may transfer the redirected benefits, the matter will not be referred to TG (Technical Group) and no further enquiries will be made.

From the HMRC *Inheritance Tax Manual*. It may be worth consulting the HMRC manual, which is available for perusal on the internet at **www.hmrc.gov.uk**. A knowledge of the HMRC position on an issue will give you an appreciation of the measures you can take which are not likely to be contentious from the HMRC perspective. (Please note that it is not being suggested that you can rely on the HMRC view of inheritance tax as gospel. There may be occasions when the HMRC position is demonstrably wrong and has to be opposed, e.g. the example of Mr Colin Lever, given at 4.4. However, it is not to be recommended that you take this as a carte blanche to challenge HMRC at every turn! In the main, you should consult professional advisors (solicitors and accountants who specialise in these areas) before challenging HMRC. You will probably find professional advice invaluable if you find yourself, as did Mr Lever, on the wrong end of a proposed fine.)

Appendix 3: Glossary

Administrator (also known as a "personal representative" or "PR")	A person who administers an estate if there is no executor to do it. This situation can arise if there is no will, or if there is a will but it fails for some reason to name an executor who is able or willing to act. (See "estate" and "probate" below.)
Appointment	The act of nominating a person to take a benefit from a trust (see "appointment, power of" below).
Appointment, power of	A power in a trust to appoint a person to take a benefit from the trust.
Business property relief (often referred to as BPR)	A relief applied to inheritance tax on certain business assets. The relief can apply at 100%, reducing the inheritance tax on the asset to nil, or at 50% reducing it to half the rate that would otherwise have been charged.
Beneficial owner/ownership	Beneficial ownership is the type of ownership that non-lawyers would usually refer to simply as ownership. It could be called "normal everyday ownership". The beneficial owner of something is the owner who is entitled to receive the entire benefit of that thing. The expression "beneficial ownership" is used to distinguish owning things as a "normal everyday owner" and owning them as a trustee.
Beneficiary	A person named in a will or trust deed who may or will receive a benefit of some kind from the will or trust deed; a person who will benefit from an estate where there is no will (an "intestate estate").
Residuary beneficiary	A beneficiary entitled to some or the entire residue of an estate. (See "residue".)
Consideration	When a contract is made, the parties to the contract each pay a price for what they receive from the other. The price is known as consideration. A deed of variation must not be for consideration.
Donor	A person who makes a gift or a transfer. This refers to a transfer made during a person's lifetime, usually a lifetime gift.

Estate	In the context of inheritance tax, wills and probate, this refers to the money, property and assets belonging to a living person, or more commonly the money, property and assets left behind by someone who has died. Note that inheritance tax may be charged at death on assets besides those which were owned by the deceased and part of his estate at death. (1.15 – PETs/chargeable transfers.)
Executor (also known as a "personal representative" or "PR")	A person named in a will to be given the responsibility of administering the estate of the testator when the testator is dead.
Gift	A transfer of money, property or assets by a person who does not receive anything of financial value in exchange for the transfer; a transfer of an asset without monetary consideration; a transfer of a gratuitous nature. (Note that when gifts are referred to in this book they will be outright gifts unless otherwise specified.)
Grant or grant of representation	This is a catch-all phrase which refers to any type of grant issued by the Probate Registry. (See "grant of probate" and "grant of representation" below).
Grant of probate	A grant of probate is the document issued by the Probate Registry when a person has died leaving a will. The grant of probate is taken as absolute proof that the persons who have proved the will (by taking it to the probate registry along with the information required by the probate registry) and are named in the grant are entitled to administer the estate. (See "probate" below.)
Grant of letters of administration	The document issued by the Probate Registry when there is no will. (See "grant of probate"). This confers authority on the persons named in it to administer the estate of the intestate. It is taken as absolute proof that the persons who are named in the grant are entitled to administer the estate. (See "intestate" and "probate" below.)

Inheritance tax (often referred to as IHT)	The name of this tax is in many ways self-explanatory. It is a tax on inheritance, or on wealth. It is charged when money, property or assets are transferred from one person to another person, or to a trust. The tax usually arises on death. However, the tax can be charged when a person transfers property during his lifetime to a trust.
Intestacy	This is the situation that arises when a person has died without leaving a will.
Intestacy, partial	This is the situation that arises when a person leaves a will which fails to dispose of all of his estate.
Intestacy, rules of	These are the rules that set out who will inherit the estate of someone who has died without leaving a valid will (i.e. has died "intestate").
Intestate	A person who has died without leaving a will. (Who may be described as "the intestate".)
Joint tenants	Joint ownership of an item of property (e.g. house or flat) by two or more people, in which they are legally treated as if they did not have separate shares in the property. Therefore, if one joint tenant dies, the surviving joint tenant or tenants automatically inherit the share of the property of the deceased joint tenant. This is known as "rights of survivorship". Rights of survivorship apply even if the deceased joint tenant makes a will purporting to give away his share of the joint property. The provision in the will giving away his share will fail to take effect because the rights of survivorship will operate to give his share to the surviving joint tenant or tenants. Houses are commonly held by married couples and civil partners as joint tenants. (See "tenants in common" and "severance of tenancy".)
Outright gift	A gift which is not subject to any conditions.
Personal representative (often abbreviated to PR)	The person who administers an estate. The expression "personal representative" can mean either an executor or an administrator.

Probate	When a person is named as executor in a will, his authority in relation to the estate stems from the will. He has wide powers as an executor, given by statute (and possibly extended by the will) to collect the money, property and assets of the deceased. However, in practice he will find that he is unable to collect many assets of the estate – possibly all of them – without a document known as a grant of probate. In particular, he will not be able to sell or transfer the house of the deceased or shares held by the deceased. The grant of probate is a document which is obtained from the probate registry by submitting an application in the correct form. When there is a death and the deceased did not leave a will, the person who is entitled to deal with his estate is known not as an executor, but as an administrator. An administrator cannot have authority conferred on him by a will, because there is no will. An administrator, in common with an executor, can apply to the Probate Registry for a grant. The grant issued to an administrator is a known as a grant of letters of administration. The administrator does not have any formal legal authority to act in the administration of an estate until he has obtained a grant of letters of administration. There are many other forms of grant that can be issued by the Probate Registry depending on the circumstances.
Qualifying interest in possession	A trust with an interest in possession which is taxed under the interest-in-possession regime rather than the relevant property regime.
Residue	That portion of an estate left over after the payment of debts, funeral expenses and testamentary expenses, legal fees and legacies.
Settlor	A person who puts money, property or assets into a trust.
Settlement	Another name for a trust
Severance of tenancy	The process by which joint tenants can become tenants in common.

Tenants in common	Joint ownership of an item of property (usually a house) by two or more people, in which each has a distinct share in the property which may be left by a will to persons other than the surviving owner or owners. This contrasts with joint tenants, who cannot dispose of their shares in jointly owned property by their wills. (See "joint tenants" and "severance of tenancy".)
Testator	A person who has made arrangements to give away his property on death by signing a will.
Testatrix	A female testator (see "testator" above).
Transfer, or transfer of value	A transfer (in the context of IHT) means the passing of legal rights, usually ownership rights, from one person to another. Value in this context means money or material worth. An easy way to understand the concept of a transfer of value is that it is what happens when you give away money, property or assets. You can give away some of your money, property and assets during your lifetime whenever you want, and you will inevitably give away all of your money, property and assets on death. Hence the tax can be charged while you are alive or on your death. The scope of a transfer of value goes beyond gifts. (See 1.2 'IHT in a nutshell' for more details and further explanation.)
Transferee	Someone who receives a transfer of value.
Transferor	Someone who makes a transfer of value.
Trust	A legal vehicle for the disposition, ownership and protection of property. The property is held by persons called trustees for the benefit of other individuals called beneficiaries. A trust can be created by a person during his lifetime or by his will on his death. (See 1.24 for more detail.)
Trust fund	Money, property or assets that are held in a trust. (See "trust" above.)

Trustees	The individuals responsible for running a trust, whether the trust is created by a will or by a trust deed (see "trust" above).
Undivided shares	Tenants in common and joint tenants are said to have "undivided shares" in the property they own, as each is entitled to occupy the whole property in common with the other owners.
Will	A statement, usually in writing, by the person making it which sets out how they would like their money, property and assets (their estate) to be given away on their death.
Will trust	A trust established by a will (see "trust" above).

Disclaimer

It bears repeating that this book does not replace the need to take legal and/or financial advice from a qualified expert when making tax-planning arrangements. Indeed, this book recommends that such advice is sought and taken.

Every effort has been made to ensure that the contents of the book are accurate when going to press. However, the accuracy of the contents cannot be guaranteed. Readers should in particular consider the issues raised in the introduction: inheritance tax, like all taxes, is frequently subject to changes.

The publisher and author and any company or individual involved in the sale or distribution of the book cannot accept responsibility for loss occasioned to any person through acting, or failing to act, as a result of relying on the contents.

Index

E

F

G

H

I

S

T

U

V

W

Other titles by Andrew Komarnyckyj

Probate Made Simple

The essential guide to saving money and getting the most out of your solicitor

Dealing with probate comes at a difficult time when a stressful legal process is particularly unwelcome. Probate can certainly appear daunting in its complexity and can be expensive in solicitors' fees, but it is possible to simplify the process and minimise the cost by taking a logical approach.

The essentials of probate work do not require special skill or expertise and it is therefore eminently feasible for most people without legal training to do the bulk of the work themselves. This means you can avoid paying expensive legal fees for select parts of the probate, making a saving of hundreds or even thousands of pounds.

Probate Made Simple, written by a solicitor with over 15 years' experience in wills and probate, sets out the detailed and specific steps to follow in order to work on probate logically, ensuring that the reader completes everything in the the right order and at the right time and that no vital stages are overlooked.

www.harriman-house.com/probatemadesimple

Available Formats:

Paperback
ISBN: 9781906659554

ePub eBook
ISBN: 9780857190147